SO-BJJ-053

Thank you Ruth for all your help
&
Thank you Jim, Becky and Mackenzie for
all your love, support and inspiration
xoxoxoxo

The opinions expressed in this manuscript are solely the opinions of the author and do not represent the opinions or thoughts of the publisher. The author has represented and warranted full ownership and/or legal right to publish all the materials in this book.

DON'T RUIN THE DOG
All Rights Reserved.
Copyright © 2014 Jill Keaton
v1.0

This book may not be reproduced, transmitted, or stored in whole or in part by any means, including graphic, electronic, or mechanical without the express written consent of the publisher except in the case of brief quotations embodied in critical articles and reviews.

Outskirts Press, Inc.
http://www.outskirtspress.com

ISBN: 978-1-4787-4023-0

Outskirts Press and the "OP" logo are trademarks belonging to Outskirts Press, Inc.

PRINTED IN THE UNITED STATES OF AMERICA

Testimonials

"My family calls Jill The Dog Whisperer. She's helped us manage all of our dogs' behavioral issues over the past 8 years by using common sense and consistency. Her training methods are not just easy but effective!"

Nancy Morrison
Concord, MA

"Jill's approach to dog training is simply wonderful! She encouraged me to look at things in a different way in order to get to the root of my dogs' behavioral problems."

Cindy Ravanis
Chelmsford, MA

"Jill is a skilled trainer who has shown us the importance of combining consistency and structure with large doses of love in order to instill confidence and achieve success in training our dog Buddy."

Susan Phillips
Acton, MA

"Our two dogs are now able to socialize with other dogs without anxiety or aggression. Rocky and Paco are much happier and we thank Jill for all her help."

Nate and Libby
Westford, MA

Table of Contents

Part 1:
Making All
The Wrong Decisions

The Story of Princess

Our story begins in Eugene Oregon, on the morning of September 1st, 2009, with the birth of Princess the Cockapoo. As the last of five puppies to be born, Princess was considered the runt of the litter, however what she lacked in size, she most certainly made up for in intelligence and sheer will.

Within hours of being born, Princess quickly began to adapt to her new world. She not only learned how to get food from her mother, but she also learned how to snuggle with her brothers and sisters in order to stay warm. In the hours and days that followed, Princess also learned that if she was the most persistent at meal time, she would get the most food and if she pushed the hardest at nap time, she would get the warmest spot in the middle of the litter. She was quickly learning how to move to the head of her pack.

Along the way she also learned about the amazing benefits of her vocalizations. From very early on, she figured out that if she used her voice, she could not only get food from her mother, but special privileges from the breeder as well. For instance, if she was lonely or cold at night, all she had to do was whimper loud and long enough, and the breeder would take her into her bed to snuggle with for the rest of the night. Life was pretty good for little Princess, who was growing bigger, stronger and smarter with each and every day that passed. Not only was she learning how to play the role of alpha dog in her litter, but she was also learning how to get everything she possibly wanted from the human in her life as well.

By week seven, Princess was the apple of her breeder's eye.

Not only would she spend countless hours in her arms each day, but anything and everything that Princess wanted, she got with just a single whimper or whine. In just a short period of time, Princess had learned that life inside her breeder's home was safe, familiar and extremely comfortable. She had everything she could possibly want and more.

Unfortunately, the sheltered life that Princess was living, would soon come to a crashing halt, when at just eight weeks old, the one person she had come to trust and rely on for everything, would have to say goodbye to her. In the early morning hours of November 1st, Princess would be placed inside a strange smelling cage called a crate, loaded into a noisy foreign object called a car and taken out into the real world for the very first time.

Having never been outside her breeder's home, everything she smelled and heard on her journey was new and strange. Fear quickly set in for Princess, but the worst was yet to come. When the car stopped, her breeder sweetly pressed her face against Princess' crate whispering soothing words and telling he that she would always love her. Without having a chance to say goodbye, Princess' crate was quickly handed off to a strange man who then brought her inside a very noisy building. Where had her breeder gone? She was all Princess had ever known. What was happening? Where was she going? Just then, her crate was handed to another new person and then another and then another. Just when she thought she couldn't take any more of the loud noises, strange smells or strange humans, her journey came to a halt. She had been placed inside the belly of an airplane that would take her to her new owner and her new home. She didn't know what was going on. All she knew was that she wanted to see her breeder. Where had she gone? As she sat in her crate, she couldn't stop shaking from fear and cold. The belly of the plane was a noisy, scary and lonely place that just kept getting scarier and noisier with every passing minute. Once all the baggage had been loaded, the doors to the cargo area were shut and Princess was plunged into complete darkness. Then the noises got even louder as the plane began its preparation for takeoff. The sounds soon became unbearable for little Princess. The plane was climbing into the sky, baggage was shifting and Princess was in near hysterics. The whimpering that began since leaving her breeder's house, had slowly increased in volume along her journey and had now transitioned to a non-stop scream for help. She began throwing herself against the door of the crate, scratching at the sides and doing anything and everything she could imagine in order to escape her hell. After ninety minutes of this behavior, Princess collapsed in a pool of her own urine and feces completely exhausted, cold, shaking from sheer terror and in extreme pain mentally and physically. After enduring nearly ten hours of cold temperatures, deafening noises and strange smells, Princess' plane began its descent into Boston. For the first time in her short life, she was away from her family and all that was familiar to her. This terribly traumatic experience would certainly scar her emotionally and change her life forever.

Once the plane touched down and Princess was juggled through more unfamiliar and strange hands and locations, she came to rest at the feet of a woman who unbeknownst to her, was Lori, her new owner. Lori couldn't believe how tiny and helpless her new little dog looked. She had no idea what Princess had just been through, but as far as she was concerned, her new little puppy was just perfect. Unable to wait any longer to hold little Princess, Lori opened the crate door and took her out to give her a big hug and kiss. Unfortunately for Lori, this decision would prove to be a messy one. Not only was the little dog covered in urine and feces from head to toe but the quick action to remove Princess from her crate caused her to nervously pee all over Lori's jacket. A horrified and embarrassed Lori quickly put Princess back into her crate in order to get her bearings. For Princess, the meet and greet was equally as frightening but no more horrific than anything else that had happened that day. By now, Princess was beyond scared, beyond exhausted, beyond hungry and beyond thirsty. Where was her breeder and when would she finally appear to save her from all of this? Why was this happening to her?

After returning Princess to her crate, Lori quickly made her way through the terminal to her SUV, not thinking of Princess and her need to drink and eliminate after being trapped in a crate for the past ten hours. As a new dog owner, Lori was not only shook up by her initial handling of Princess, but overwhelmed by the puppies' state of being. Lori quickly made her way back to her vehicle and loaded Princess' crate into the front passenger seat, so she could keep and eye on her little puppy. Once again, Princess found herself in a noisy, strange smelling car with a strange new human. Princess was wet, scared, exhausted, hungry, thirsty and extremely confused. Unable to relax, Princess did what always worked to bring her good things and that was to whine. Despite her sheer exhaustion, Princess managed to shake and whine in desperation for the next hour and a half, hoping to be saved from this never-ending nightmare.

Once home, Lori wasted no time in getting Princess into the house and into the kitchen sink to wash away the urine and feces that covered her entire body. After about thirty minutes of scrubbing and rubbing and blow-drying, Princess looked like a new girl. Lori couldn't help but marvel at how beautiful her little baby looked. After giving her a bunch of hugs and kisses,

Lori decided to let her get acquainted with her new home and investigate the kitchen while she ran to the bathroom to get cleaned up.

For Princess it was the first time she'd been on her feet and outside of her crate in nearly fourteen hours. Being an eight-week-old puppy with an extremely full bladder, it was only a matter of minutes before she stopped to take a nice long pee on the kitchen floor. Once she relieved herself she began to whine, in hopes that Lori would return to the kitchen. Luckily for Princess, Lori was just as much of a sucker for her vocalizations as her breeder had been and quickly returned to the kitchen to scooped her up and comfort her with hugs and kisses. Although she was still a little unsure of Lori, she was the only human available to care for her and give her what she wanted.

Lori was just so happy to have her little baby nice and clean, that she didn't even notice that Princess had peed on the kitchen floor, until she stepped in it. Feeling bad for the nervous little dog, Lori quickly and quietly cleaned up the mess to avoid making Princess feel bad about the mistake.

For the rest of the evening, Lori would enjoy showering Princess with toys, treats and attention in hopes of making her feel happy and loved. The way Lori saw it, what harm could come from treating her little Princess like a princess.

Before retiring to bed, Lori decided to call her husband Kurt, who was traveling for work, and fill him in on her hectic day. She told Kurt all about how adorable Princess was and how she couldn't wait for him to meet her. Lori was certain that this little puppy would help them fill the void they felt from not being able to have a child.

After hanging up with Kurt, Lori decided it was time for them both to go to bed. Unfortunately for Lori, her attempts to put Princess in her crate for the night were met with great protest. After struggling with Princess for nearly ten minutes, she figured it would be much easier to just let Princess sleep with her on her bed for the night. What harm could come from one night on the bed she thought.

By 6 a.m. Lori was amazed that Princess had made it through the night without even a whimper. She had found a comfortable spot on Kurt's pillow and was curled up like a ball. How cute, Lori thought. The happy thoughts were soon interrupted when Lori looked down at the bottom of the bed to find a small pile of poop. She hadn't even heard or felt Princess stir in the night, so how could this have happened? Lori assumed that this was normal behavior for puppies and figured it wasn't worth getting upset over, just yet. She had plenty of supplies to clean things up, so this would be no problem.

After cleaning up the night's mess without disturbing Princess, Lori decided to jump in the shower, while her little puppy slept. Once Princess stirred and realized she was all alone in the room, she began to whimper and whine. Where had Lori gone? Had she left me too? In her fit of anxiety, Princess began to pee. How could she get off this bed? It seemed so high and she was just so scared. Instead of jumping down, she just decided to whine even louder in hopes that Lori would come and save her. Sure enough, Lori having heard the commotion from the shower, burst out of the bathroom and ran to Princess. "It's all right baby, Mommy won't leave you alone again," was what Lori told Princess over and over again, while rocking her. After ten minutes of this, Lori was able to calm Princess down to the point where she stopped shaking and was now licking the side of her face. Lori felt relieved to have gotten past this and knew she would need to devote a lot more love and attention to this little girl in order to make her feel safe. She knew she'd have her work cut out for her, but if she was willing to care for a baby, she was convinced she could care for a dog.

For the next few days, Lori would continue to lavish Princess with more new toys, yummy treats and excessive attention. She soon realized that the best way to keep Princess from freaking out was to keep her by her side at all times. This even meant bringing her into the bathroom with her when she had to use the toilet, take a shower, put on makeup or brush her teeth. No matter what Lori did or where Lori went, Princess was right there. Lori didn't mind the constant companionship; after all, a four thousand square foot home was a pretty lonely place when Kurt was away. Now she had Princess to keep her company and happily everything she was doing seemed to be helping to make her happy, calm and well adjusted. Lori felt proud of the progress she had made and was excited about her new life with little Princess.

On day five, Lori was full of excitement because today was the day she would take her little Princess to the vet. All she could think about was how fun it would be to take her baby out for their first adventure together. Figuring that the crate would just upset little Princess, Lori decided to put her on the passenger's seat, where she could keep an eye on her and comfort her if necessary. Unfortunately, as soon as the car began to move, Princess began to panic. She wanted nothing to do with the passenger's seat and quickly jumped across the armrest onto Lori's lap. Here she would remain for the next 15 minutes, shaking and whining until they reached the vet's office.

Once they arrived, Lori was hopeful that things would improve. Maybe it was just the association with the car and the airport experience that freaked Princess out. Either way, this wasn't going to stop her. With Princess snuggled deep into the crook of her arm, Lori headed inside. From the minute she opened the door and stepped inside the vet's office, Princess began to shake and whine. Lori tried to console her, but it was no use. The strange dogs barking, the unfamiliar smells and the constant flow of people passing by her in the waiting room, made her shake and whine even more.

After spending what felt like an eternity in the waiting room, Lori and Princess were finally escorted into an examining room. There they met with Dr. Kelly, a sweet, compassionate woman and a seasoned pro with nervous dogs. She had a kind way about her, but Princess wanted nothing to do with her and simply shook while standing on the cold steel exam table. After wailing through the entire exam, that included three puppy shots and a blood draw, everything was finally over. Dr. Kelly could see that Lori was equally shook up by the event and simply reminded her that Princess was still very young. "Get her out to see the world and all that it has to offer over the next few months," said Dr. Kelly. Lori thanked the doctor for her patience and promised to get Princess out more in the months ahead. Once they exited the exam room, Lori went straight to the front desk to pay her bill. Lori felt pretty embarrassed due to the fact that so many patients in the waiting room were staring at her and Princess, most likely because of all the noise that had come from their exam room. She clutched the shaking Princess even closer and tried to sooth her by telling her they would be going home now and that everything would be ok. When she got Princess out to the car, she broke down and cried over how difficult and embarrassing the last forty-five minutes had been. With Princess curled up and still shaking in her lap, they both headed home to recover.

Much to Lori's relief, Princess showed instant improvement once they got back home. It was as if a switch had been flipped. Princess perked up and seemed back to normal, once she saw she was back inside her safe place. Lori and Princess both stayed inside for the rest of the day exhausted and defeated from their morning's misadventure. Princess was content to stay glued to Lori's lap for the next few hours and Lori was just so happy to see her little baby back to normal.

Over the next few days, Lori would try to expose Princess to new things, by going on walks up and down the street. The walks were very slow going, as Princess seemed startled by anything and everything, including hydrants, rustling leaves, birds, her own leash and especially cars. Anytime a car would pass by, Princess would go into a frenzy of yelping and intense pulling to run back to the house. It seemed as if anything and everything frightened Princess. Lori knew that the walks were necessary, but boy was she glad when they were over. They were just as grueling for her, as they were for her little baby, but she would not be defeated. She had invested too much time and money to just throw in the towel. She had to stay positive, especially since Kurt would be returning home later that day.

After spending the morning giving the house a thorough cleaning and making sure Princess looked and smelled just perfect, Lori was ready for Kurt to arrive. From the moment he walked through the door, Princess was on edge. Kurt was the first male that she had ever come in direct contact with and the fact that he was now trying to touch her, threw her into a state of panic. Lori could see that Princess was upset and rather than let it escalate, she simply picked her up to hug her and tell her that everything was ok. Kurt asked Lori what was wrong, and Lori simply said, "Oh she's just a bit shy, she'll get over it." Since the last thing Kurt wanted to do was upset his little puppy, he decided it would be best to give her plenty of room so he left the room to go upstairs and unpack. Within a half hour of being home, Kurt asked Lori why the house had a strange smell to it. Regretfully, Lori explained to Kurt that Princess wasn't quite housetrained, just yet, but that she was doing her best to keep up with Princess' mistakes. He was a little upset at the thought that he was living in Princess' outhouse, but Lori simply reminded him that she was still just a puppy and would grow out of it eventually.

When it came time for bed, Kurt was surprised to find that he no longer had a pillow. His pillow had now become Princess' bed. Lori got a good chuckle out of telling Kurt that she'd have to get him a new one in the morning because he couldn't take away Princess' bed at bedtime. Needless to say the only one to go to bed that night without a pillow, was Kurt. Despite this inconvenience, Kurt had to laugh, thinking how this little dog had clearly taken over the house.

The next day Kurt would find out more about Princess and her fears, when he attempted to take her on a walk around the neighborhood. Kurt was surprised to find that Princess was afraid of just about everything in the outside world. No wonder Lori was having such a hard time getting her to go to the bathroom outside, she basically feared the outside world all together. When he returned from his walk, Kurt explained what had happened to Lori, but she was hardly surprised. She reluctantly told him how upset she gets on walks, riding in the car, visiting strange places, hearing loud noises and meeting new people and new dogs. Lori explained that Princess had been that way since day one and that she hoped she would just grow out of it. Being concerned that Princess may need help, Lori asked Kurt if they should seek professional assistance, but being someone who liked to figure things out for himself, Kurt assured Lori that he would do some research and figure out how to fix their little Princess. The way he saw it, why pay a trainer for advice that you could get from a bunch of books or from the Internet. Never being one to go against her husband's decisions, Lori simply trusted him and hoped he would do what was best for Princess.

Over the next few months, Kurt did his best to read and surf the net looking for advice on how to deal with Princess' anxieties. He tried dozens of different approaches, but nothing seemed to be working. If anything, Princess was getting worse and both Kurt and Lori were losing their motivation. To make matters worse, both Kurt and Lori were using different approaches in trying to fix Princess. While Kurt demonstrated a tough love approach, Lori believed in coddling and supporting Princess when she demonstrated any fear or anxiety. This was very frustrating for both of them and as a result Princess was getting out less and her opportunities to interact with new people, places, things and dogs were becoming few and far between. Lori didn't think it was such a bad thing to keep Princess close to home, after all it was the middle of winter and she didn't prefer to be out in the freezing cold either. The way she saw it, she would just have to play a bit of catch up in the spring and summer, when social opportunities were more readily and easily available. In Lori's eyes, Princess was more than just a timid little dog. She was a wonderful companion. Lori enjoyed Princess' company and truly loved her, even if she refused to sit, come, lie down or use her wee pads on a consistent basis. Princess had proven to be a real handful, but Lori just figured they were typical puppy behaviors that she would eventually grow out of.

After what seemed like a very long winter, spring had finally sprung and it was time to get Princess out to see the real world. For their first outing, Lori thought it would be a good idea to take Princess to the local dog park, to not only see some new things, but make some new friends as well. She'd be on her own with Princess, since Kurt was on the road for work, but

this didn't bother Lori, after all, she preferred her style of training over Kurt's less compassionate approach. She hated to see
her baby upset and always figured it was her job as her mother
and guardian to sooth her worries and make her feel safe and
calm. She saw today as a new start and was excited to get going.
After gathering up a few supplies, they were off. Lori loaded
Princess into the SUV, where she would remain shaking in her
lap until they reached their destination. She had hoped that
after a half dozen car rides, Princess would feel a bit more comfortable in the car, but like everything else, she now just hoped
she'd grow out of it. After a ten-minute ride, they had reached
the dog park. Lori was very excited to see dozens of cars in the
parking lot, indicating that there would be plenty of dogs for
little Princess to meet. After leashing Princess and carrying her
into the park, Lori gently placed her baby down on the ground
where she was immediately approached by several curious and
friendly dogs. This was the first time Princess had come nose
to nose with one strange dog, let alone four. Her immediate
reaction was to tuck her tail between her legs and shake in fear.
When this didn't work to make them go away, she gave them
a growl and when that didn' t work, she snapped repeatedly at
them, until they all backed away. At that moment, a terribly
embarrassed and concerned Lori scooped little Princess up into
her arms and began telling her everything was all right. She was
surprised at Princess' reaction, given that she normally would
just shutter and whine when she was faced with something
new or scary. Never had she growled or tried to bite out of
fear. Although this was the first time she had ever seen Princess
around other dogs, she was just shocked at how her little baby
had reacted. A sympathetic dog owner quickly came to Lori's
side, feeling concerned for what she had just witnessed. Her
dog was one of the dogs Princess had snapped at, but she felt

compelled to try and help Lori and her frightened little dog. As a dog owner of twenty-five years, Katie had a tremendous amount of experience with dogs of all ages and hoped that Lori would let her help her through this ordeal. "How old is your puppy?" Katie asked an obviously shook up Lori. "She's nine months old," Lori replied. "Has she ever been around other dogs?" "No not really," Lori answered. With just this brief exchange of information, Katie knew that she was dealing with a very inexperienced dog owner and felt compelled to offer her a bit of advice. Unfortunately, before she could say anything else, Lori and Princess had hightailed it out of the park and back to their SUV. Once inside her vehicle, Lori began to sob uncontrollably. She was so disappointed, so embarrassed and yet so concerned about her little Princess. She hugged and kissed Princess telling her repeatedly that everything would be all right, but not really knowing if in fact it would be. How was she going to deal with what had just happened? She had never seen Princess act this way. How could she take her to the dog park again if she was going to attack other dogs? What if she had bitten one of the other dogs and that owner had threatened to sue her? How would she explain that to Kurt? After she got her emotions under control, Lori sped out of the parking lot and headed home.

Once at home Lori called Kurt and told him about what had happened. Needless to say, he was not very happy. He had told Lori to get Princess out to meet new people, places and things, but the advice had fallen on deaf ears over the past seven months. He had also told Lori that Princess was a dog, not a baby, and needed to be treated as such. He knew that Lori had always wanted kids and since receiving the news from her doctor that children would most likely not be in their future, he had tried to be sympathetic and understanding about her new relationship with Princess. He knew that Princess was filling a void for Lori, but he also didn't want her to be creating a nightmare that neither one of them could live with. Being so far away from home on a business trip, Kurt's last words of advice to Lori were to go into his office and read through some of the dog training books he had on his desk. "It can't hurt to take a look at what they have to say," he said. Lori agreed and thanked Kurt for his advice and for being so understanding. After hanging up with her husband, Lori went into his office and read a few of the book jackets to figure out which book sounded best to her. Although she was reluctant to change her loving approach toward Princess, she thought she owed it to Kurt to read at least one of the books he had purchased.

By the next day, Lori had finished reading the book she had chosen and was pretty anxious to try out what she had learned on a walk with Princess. Unfortunately, Lori was met with the usual resistance. Throughout the walk, Princess repeatedly tried to run back to the house whenever a leaf would blow, a car would pass or she would see her own shadow. Like all the walks before, this one was a battle, but Lori was not going to give up and head back home so easily this time. She told Princess that she was going to have to work through her fears before they were going to head back home, even if it took all day. Despite nearly two hours of offering Princess treats as distractions and praise for any type of forward movement, a defeated Lori decided it was time to head back home. She had failed. Not only was Lori completely exhausted, but she was completely frustrated. She felt as though she'd tried everything, but nothing seemed to work. Maybe Princess wasn't meant to go outside. Maybe she wasn't meant to ride in a car. Maybe she wasn't meant to hang out with strange people or strange dogs in strange places. Maybe it would be easier to just keep her at home. After all, she was perfectly content at home. Maybe things would be a whole lot easier if she just gave in and let Princess have her way. She obviously wasn't going to change, so why fight a losing battle? She realized her will wasn't nearly as strong as Princess' and that she was always much quicker to give up when things weren't going her way. She was at an absolute loss. What was she going to do? Kurt would be home in a few days, so she figured she'd just take it easy until he returned.

For Princess, indoor living was what she preferred. She always had a knack for getting what she wanted and this would be not exception. In her eyes, the humans were always the first to fold. If she stood her ground long enough, they would give in and she would get her way. Princess was all about being able to control her surroundings. When she was home, she was familiar with everything and knew how to control most every aspect of her environment. When she was outdoors, there were too many uncontrollable variables for her to feel comfortable. For Princess, control equaled comfort.

After nearly three weeks away, Kurt finally returned home and Lori was never so happy to see him. Kurt loved his wife and was just as happy to see her and be back home. In a funny way, Kurt couldn't blame Princess; he too enjoyed the comforts and safety of home. Once Kurt got settled in, he sat down with Lori to find out how things were going with Princess and most importantly, if she was still happy with her little dog. Lori assured Kurt that she was truly happy with Princess and that she was especially happy that she had finally been able to potty train Princess to her indoor wee pads. This was no easy feat, but she had done it, and she hoped to accomplish more. Lori explained to Kurt that she loved everything about Princess when they were together in the home; it was just outside of the home that she became a handful. Lori knew that Princess was obviously a high maintenance dog, but she told Kurt that she didn't mind this. She explained to him that she enjoyed caring and catering to her endless demands, but that she had lost the motivation to take her out of the house and challenge her fears. Kurt explained that as long as she was happy, so was he. He just wanted to make sure that Lori was ok with the limitations that Princess had put on Lori as a dog owner and as a human. Lori knew that Princess was the one calling the shots, but she was ok with it, after all Princess was her little baby.

Over the next several months, Lori would find great happiness with having Kurt at home. For the first time in nearly a year, he was not traveling and in Lori's eyes, it was just what the two of them needed. Even Princess was happy having Kurt around the house. The three of them were finally enjoying time together as a family. Just when they thought things couldn't get any better, they did. Lori's visit to the doctor revealed that she was two weeks pregnant; despite the fact that countless doctors had said they couldn't get pregnant. Kurt and Lori were over the moon with joy. They had wanted a baby for years, but thought it would never happen. How did it happen they thought? Could Princess have brought them this good fortune? Either way, their family would be expanding and they couldn't be any happier.

Lori and Kurt were in seventh heaven for several weeks, until Kurt received word that he would be heading back out on the road for work. Unfortunately for Lori, she would soon begin experiencing the nausea, exhaustion, headaches and food aversions that would plague her for the next three month. She was becoming mentally and physically exhausted on a daily basis and without Kurt around, she was finding it difficult to cater to both her needs and the needs of Princess. Finding the energy to get Princess a treat, anytime she barked at the treat cabinet, which was often 10-15 times a day, was beginning to get more difficult. Finding the energy to play fetch with Princess, each time she demanded it, which was often 20-30 times a day, was beginning to get more difficult. Finding the energy to carry her around the house and then lavish her with attention on her lap throughout the day was also beginning to get more difficult. Princess' world was changing by the day and she did not like it in the least. She had grown accustomed to being a dog who's constant demands were always met. Why was Lori acting so difficult she thought? Princess had always gotten what she wanted when she wanted, so she always assumed she was in charge. Her control over her environment was slowly slipping and lack of control was making her anxious and unhappy.

Before long, Lori began finding little messes throughout the house. These messes were not only happening in the kitchen and living room, but in her bedroom and on her bed as well. It was as if Princess wanted to be sure that Lori found these messes. At first, Lori thought the messes were minor setbacks in Princess' wee pad training, but after two weeks of finding little presents scattered throughout the house, she was beginning to wonder if it was Princess' way of acting out. Over the course of the next few weeks and months, Princess would begin acting out in ways that Lori could never have imagined. For instance, one afternoon while Princess was napping on the couch, Lori's attempted to move her to the floor was met with great protest. Princess did not like being disturbed by a lower ranking pack member and made this clear to Lori by growling and snapping at her. At first, Lori was upset, but after giving is some thought, she figured maybe it was her fault for having disturbed her while she was sleeping. Not wanting to wake her again, Lori abandoned her attempt to nap on the couch and simply went upstairs to rest on her bed. For Princess, this was an act of defiance that made her feel empowered. She had stated her dominance over Lori and won. Princess would soon demonstrate another act of dominance, while sleeping on Lori's bed. One evening, while experiencing yet another night of restless sleep, Lori attempted to make more room for herself on the bed by moving Princess. Unfortunately for Lori, this would prove to be a big mistake. No sooner did Lori begin to lift Princess that she turned and snapped at Lori, this time breaking the skin. For Princess, it was simply another statement of defiance and dominance aimed at Lori, a lower ranking pack member. A visibly shaken and distraught Lori raced to the bathroom to tend to her bleeding hand, while Princess simply watched from the comfort of her throne. Again, Lori assumed it was her fault for trying to move a sleeping dog and rather than confront Princess, Lori simply went downstairs to sleep on the couch for the rest of the night. Lori couldn't understand why Princess was acting this way. She couldn't imagine that Princess would knowingly try to hurt her. They were best friends and loved one another, so why was this happening?

Unfortunately, the outbursts would continue when a friend of Lori's would stop by a few days later to see how she was doing with her pregnancy. Because Lori knew that Princess felt uncomfortable around strangers, she thought it would be a good idea to have Karen let Princess sniff her hand upon greeting her at the front door. Unfortunately, this would prove to be a bad decision. Rather than interpret Karen's action as a sign of peace, Princess took it as a threat and quickly nipped Karen on the hand. Naturally, Lori was horrified at what she had just witnessed and quickly scooped up Princess to get her away from her friend. With trembling hands and a shaky voice, Lori attempted to reprimand Princess by saying "Princess that was wrong, very, very wrong." After scolding Princess, Lori asked Karen if she was ok? Karen, who was equally as shocked, excused herself to the bathroom where she tended to her minor puncture wound and regained her composure. Lori, who held Princess in her arms for fear of another incident, could not apologize enough. She told Karen that she knew Princess was nervous around strangers, but had never seen her act aggressively. The last thing Karen wanted to do was to upset her friend so early on in her pregnancy, so she told her she was fine and then made an excuse to exit. Once Karen was out the door, Lori completely broke down. She sobbed and asked Princess over and over again why she would do such a thing, all the while cradling her in her arms. Filled with worry, Lori would not sleep that night. All she could think about was how Kurt would react to all of this and most importantly, what would Princess be like with the new baby? What would she do? After a night of tossing and turning, Lori decided that the best thing to do would be to keep all of this from Kurt, in order to avoid possibly losing her darling Princess.

Over the last remaining months of Lori's pregnancy, she would do her best to juggle her responsibilities of taking care of Princess, taking care of herself and getting the house ready for a baby. With Kurt constantly on the road, she had her hands full with all these responsibilities, but she felt that the most important task was keeping Princess happy and trying not to disturb her normal everyday routine and activities. She certainly didn't want to experience any more of Princess' outbursts, so if anything, she was catering even more to Princess' needs than she was her own. She was even doing her best to hide all the baby things that were coming into the house, so as not to make Princess nervous. She knew strange things could sometimes spook Princess, so in order to avoid any problems, she just kept everything in the baby's room with the door shut. Again, Kurt had no idea what was really going on, but in Loris' mind, what he didn't know, couldn't hurt him.

Finally the big day arrived. Luckily Kurt was home on a three-week break from the road and was right by Lori's side when her water broke. Before heading to the hospital, Kurt and Lori grabbed their pre-packed bags and settled Princess into her exercise pen with plenty of food, water and wee pads. After seven long hours of labor, Kurt and Lori welcomed their little girl Hope into the world. She was 6 lbs. 10 oz. and every bit the new love of their lives. They were both so overwhelmed with the excitement of the event that it wasn't until nearly five hours later that they thought about Princess. Lori assured Kurt that she and Hope were fine and sent him home to check on her. Thankfully, the hospital was only fifteen minutes away, so Kurt was able to make several trips back and forth to tend to Princess over the next two days. With each visit, Princess looked more and more unhappy. She had never been left alone for such a long period of time. All her basic needs were being met, but she had lost complete control of everything and she was not happy. Kurt could tell that Princess was unhappy, but the last thing he was going to do, was convey this to Lori, while she was recuperating.

After two long days at the hospital, Kurt and Lori were finally able to bring little Hope home to introduce to Princess. All Lori could think about was how happy she would be to have her family all together. After bringing in all the baggage and baby supplies, Kurt had Lori go into the kitchen to greet Princess, while he took Hope straight into the nursery. Lori and Princess were so happy to see each other that the two cuddled and exchanged kisses for nearly ten minutes straight. Their re-union was eventually interrupted by the sound of little Hope crying in the nursery. As soon as Princess heard this strange sound, she jumped from Lori's arms and tore down the hall toward the nursery, all the while barking at the top of her lungs. This strange noise was coming from within her home and she was going to find out what it was. Once Princess reached the nursery door, she threw herself against it and raced inside, barking and growling. Without giving it a second thought, she immediately lunged at Kurt, while he held a crying Hope in his arms. Kurt, who wanted nothing more than to protect his newborn baby, instantly reacted by pushing Princess aside with his leg. This however, would not stop Princess. She was in a zone of panic and anxiety and would continue to bark, growl and leap up at a crying Hope, even after Lori burst into the room. With Princess barking and Kurt yelling at Lori to get Princess out of the room, Lori quickly reached down to grab Princess, only to be bitten by a dog who was in no mood to be dictated to. At that point, Kurt took over. He had seen enough and with one swift kick, knocked Princess out of the room and into the hallway. Kurt then slammed the nursery door, gently placed a crying Hope into her bassinet and then went to Lori's side to help her tend to her wound. Princess had bitten her on her right index finger and it was now bleeding onto the nursery floor. Kurt wrapped her hand in a baby blanket and raced her out to the kitchen to wash away the blood. Much to Lori and Kurt's relief, the cut was not too deep and after a thorough washing, only required a few Band-Aids for covering. Once the wound had been cared for, Lori went back to the nursery to check on Hope. Lori could hear Kurt scolding Princess in the kitchen, followed by a loud demand that she get in her pen. Shortly thereafter, Kurt returned to the nursery to see if everything was all right. "What in the world just happened?" Kurt asked Lori. "I don't know," Lori responded. She didn't think this was a good time to tell Kurt about Princess' other outbursts, but now she knew she had a big problem on her hands. What was she going to do? Kurt was absolutely disgusted with Princess and did everything in his power to not even look at her for the rest of the night. Lori on the other hand, felt horrible that Princess had reacted so negatively to Hope's crying. She also felt guilty for not having sought professional advice for Princess' aggression when it first surface, so many months ago. Maybe all of this could have been avoided. Either way, she felt responsible for what had just happened and just hoped it wouldn't happen again.

After several days home with Hope, Kurt and Lori were beginning to fall into a sleep deprived routine. Like all new parents, they felt a bit overwhelmed, but the joy they were experiencing with Hope, far outweighed everything else. As for Princess, Kurt felt it was best to keep her in her exercise pen until the newness of the baby wore off. It wasn't until nearly three and a half days later, that Princess was allowed out of her exercise pen to investigate her surroundings. At first, Princess was watched with a close eye, but as the hours and days passed, she was given more freedom and more attention. After only a week's time, Princess was back in Lori's good graces. Lori couldn't help but feel bad for all that Princess had been through and as a result, began giving her everything she wanted, when she wanted, like old times. Even Kurt had begun to forgive Princess, thinking she had come to accept little Hope, by the fact that she no longer seemed agitated by her presence. The peace however, would not last for long.

After getting settled in for what Lori and Kurt hoped would be a quiet night at home, Lori decided to watch television, while feeding Hope. With her newborn swaddled in a thick blanket, Lori decided to settle down on the couch, to enjoy a bit of comfort. She didn't think twice about this decision, despite the fact that Princess was napping on the couch, only a few feet away. Kurt, who was close by in the kitchen preparing dinner, didn't seem concerned either. After all, Princess had seemingly come to accept Hope and should have been ok with sharing the couch with her. Unfortunately for Hope, she would soon be the target of yet another one of Princess' outbursts. Within moments of the two settling down on the couch, all it would take would be an innocent little cry from Hope to awaken Princess and trigger an attack. Princess, who felt she was protecting Lori from this concealed threat, reacted by latching onto the blanket and pulling it away from Lori. As soon as it happened, Lori began screaming, as Princess began tearing at the blanket that held her precious newborn. At that moment, Kurt raced into the living room to find Princess in a frenzy of aggression, aimed at his daughter Hope. He instantly began screaming at Princess, while trying to push her away with his hand. Unfortunately, no sooner did Princess let go of Hope that she latched onto Kurt's forearm. She remembered what Kurt had done to her in the nursery and would make every attempt to defend herself this time. Kurt then grabbed Princess by the scruff; despite the pain he was experiencing in his forearm and raced to the kitchen, to drop Princess into her exercise pen. She had given him a good puncture wound, but nothing was going to prevent him from protecting his wife and child. "That's it!" Kurt screamed, while racing back to Lori and Hope. "That dog is out of here!" A horrified and stunned Lori could only look on in fright, as Kurt grabbed their screaming child from her arms to examine her for injuries. After unwrapping the blanket, Kurt found that Hope was completely uninjured. Thankfully, Princess had only latched onto the blanket and nothing else. After seeing that Hope was unscathed, Kurt broke down into tears while holding his baby. With a cracked voice, he told Lori that Princess had to go. Kurt could not take any more of Princess' outbursts. Lori, who was in shock, could only stare at Hope in disbelief. How could she have let it get to this? How could Princess have done this? What was she going to do without her little Princess? She knew this was the last straw for Kurt and frankly, it was just about all that Lori could take as well.

It would take nearly three hours before Kurt and Lori were able to recover from their shock. With Hope fast asleep in her bassinet, Lori broke down and told Kurt about the other instances when Princess had acted out toward her and her friend Karen. Kurt was furious that she hadn't told him about these outbursts. "How could you not tell me?" he said. "What if Hope had been injured or even killed by Princess?" Lori agreed that keeping this information from him was wrong and just plain stupid. Lori stayed up most of the night sobbing and coming to terms with the fact that she had to find another home for Princess. She just could not stay with them any longer. She was simply too dangerous to have around a baby.

Early the next morning, Kurt would head off to work determined to find someone to take Princess off their hands. Before leaving, Kurt gave Lori strict orders not to let Princess out of her pen while he was gone. She assured him that this would not be a problem. Lori tried to keep herself busy throughout the day, so as to avoid contact with Princess, who was clearly aware that things were not ok. Princess would remain in her pen shaking and whining throughout the day, hoping to gain back control of her environment by expressing extreme anxiety and fear. Princess knew that this had always worked in the past, so why wasn't it working now?

This would prove to be a very long day for everyone, but

when Kurt returned home from work that evening, he had good news. He had found a new home for Princess. After spreading the word at his office of more than 250 employees, about needing to find a home for Princess, he had been approached by Alice, a woman who was interested in adopting her. Kurt told Lori that Alice was a sweet, middle-aged woman, who lived alone and would be able to provide Princess with a good home. Lori was happy that Kurt had been able to find a good home for Princess, but did it have to happen so quickly? Kurt explained that it would be best for everyone if he took the next day off and brought Princess to Alice's home, to allow them to meet and begin their new life together. Despite Lori's sadness for having to give up Princess, she was happy to know that she was going to a good home. Kurt assured Lori that he had known Alice for many years and that she was a wonderfully sweet woman, who would be able to give Princess a loving, low stress life. Kurt assured Lori that this would be the best solution for everyone and it would allow Princess to live happily ever after.

Knowing that Kurt had already made up his mind, Lori sadly spent the rest of the evening gathering up all of Princess' belongings to go to her new home with Alice. Once she was done putting everything into bags by the door, Lori went upstairs to cry. She couldn't help but wonder where she had gone wrong as a dog owner. She'd given Princess everything she wanted, so why was she so unhappy? Why hadn't she seen this coming? Why had she seemed to get more aggressive the older she got? Why was she such a fearful dog? The questions just kept coming and she had no answers. She loved Princess dearly, but could no longer protect her. Princess had crossed a line with Kurt and there was no turning back. The only thing that could comfort Lori was the thought that she would have a good home with Alice and that she would be loved.

When morning finally arrived, Kurt loaded up the car with all of Princess' belongings, while Lori said her last goodbyes. She told Princess how much she loved her and how she was so sorry for not having been able to do enough to help her. She told her that Alice would take good care of her and that she would check in on her often, to make sure she was doing ok. She gave her a big hug and kiss and then loaded her into the same crate she had arrived in, nearly two years ago to the day. Kurt told Lori everything would be ok and that is was time for him to take Princess. Sobbing uncontrollably, Lori said goodbye to Princess and watched as Kurt took her into the garage and loaded her into the SUV. Lori watched Kurt drive away with Princess and couldn't help but feel like this was all her fault. She loved that little dog and had just wished that things had turned out differently.

As Kurt drove away, he knew that what he was doing would be the best thing for everyone, especially little Hope. With Princess whining inside her crate in the back seat, Kurt felt little to no guilt as he pulled into their vet's parking lot.

Unfortunately for Princess, there was no Alice. He had made up the whole story, because without it, he never would have been able to get Princess out of the house and away from his defenseless newborn baby. He had spoken to the vet the day before and after much discussion between the two, it was decided that the best thing to do would be to put Princess to sleep. Princess had a history of biting humans and most likely, this would only get worse. The way Kurt saw it, Princess' anxieties and aggressive tendencies made her a danger, not only to those around her, but to society as well. Kurt felt horrible about having to lie to Lori, but what she didn't know, couldn't hurt her. Kurt would never tell her what he had done.

Once inside the vet's office, Kurt was quickly ushered into an examining room, where Dr. Sampson was waiting. Because everything had been discussed between Dr. Sampson and Kurt the day before, there was little to be said between the two. With the consent form signed, Dr. Sampson reached into the crate to take Princess out and in typical fashion, she bit the hand that threatened her. Dr. Sampson recoiled and instantly looked at Kurt as if to say, you are making the right decision. With a bit more caution, Dr. Sampson proceeded to remove Princess from her crate and muzzle her, to prevent her from doing further damage to him or his staff. At that point, Dr. Sampson administered the shot that quickly and painlessly caused her to pass away. Kurt said goodbye to a limp Princess and deep inside, he told her he was sorry. Like Lori, he wondered if there was more he could have done. Should he have insisted on getting professional help to address her anxieties, rather than trying to fix them himself? He questioned everything, just as Lori had done, but unfortunately, there was nothing either of them could do, Princess was gone.

After taking the rest of Princess' things to the local animal shelter as a donation, Kurt headed home. He was full of guilt, but he would never let Lori know what he had done. In his mind, he did what was best for his family.

Part 2: Making All
The Right Decisions

Introduction

Like Princess the Cockapoo, all too many dogs in this country are being ruined in one way or another by the people who should be taking care of them. These owners may have good intentions, but unfortunately for the dogs, the end results are often pretty negative. Dogs who are acquired to fill a void, are often the dogs who suffer the most. These dogs are unwillingly molded into neurotic, fearful, under socialized, anxiety ridden and/or aggressive dogs, who are this way, because one or more humans have trained them to be this way.

As a dog trainer for the past thirteen years and the owner of a doggie daycare, I have seen my share of these dogs. The sad thing is, most owners have no idea they are in fact contributing to their dog's behavioral issues and those who realize they are at fault have no idea what to do to fix their mistakes. I try to explain to these owners that a dog will only do what his or her environment allows them to get away with and the only way the dog will change, is if the owner/environment changes.

It is my hope that the information provided in this book will help dog owners to make better decisions, not only in regards to how to choose a dog breed, but how to pick the right dog breeder and how to raise a healthy, happy and confident dog. I also hope this book will help dog owners realize how important it is that they make the right decisions about raising their canine companions and that they take their job as teacher, translator and guide, very seriously, so as to create a dog that is not only a joy to have around the house, but a joy to bring out in public as well.

Topic 1:
Choosing The Right Breed

Choosing the right breed of dog is a big decision that should not be taken lightly. All too often, people will go by looks when choosing a breed. This can be a part of the decision process, but by no means should it be the main reason for choosing a particular breed of dog. Instead, choose a breed that best matches your personality and lifestyle. Whether you will be getting a dog from a breeder or a shelter, be sure to extensively research each breed you are interested in ahead of time and most importantly, do not base your decision on guilt or impulse. Otherwise, you could end up taking home the *wrong dog.*

The first thing you'll want to do as you begin your search for the "perfect dog" is to finding out which breeds are right for you and your environment. One way to do this is to take a breed selector quiz. These helpful quizzes can be found by conducting an Internet search using the keywords:

breed selector quiz

*Don't limit yourself to just one breed. Find a few breeds that you are compatible with so you'll have more dogs to choose from.

Once you have taken a breed selector quiz and you have the list of dogs that you are compatible with, it will then be a good idea to gather as much information as possible about each breed that is on your list. This information may be obtained by visiting your local library, bookstore or by conducting a breed specific search on the Internet.

The following list of questions will be helpful to you as you embark on your fact- finding mission. These questions will allow you to narrow down your search as you attempt to find the breeds that are truly best suited to you and your environment:

- **What characteristics define the breed?**

- **What behavioral issues are unique to the breed?**

- **What does the breed demand for grooming and exercise?**

- **How much does the breed shed?**

- **Is the breed good with kids and/or other animals?**

- **Is the breed a social or independent breed?**

- **Is the breed prone to aggression?**

- **Is the breed extremely vocal?**

- Does the breed exhibit watch dog or guard dog tendencies?

- What is the typical lifespan of the breed?

- Is the breed prone to any medical conditions?

- How big does the breed typically get when full grown as a male or as a female?

- How much will it cost to feed a dog of this particular breed each week?

- Will a dog of this breed affect your heath or the health of a family member who may suffer from allergies?

- How big is your yard and is it fenced?

- How much time will the dog be alone each day?

The more you know about each breed, the better. Surprises will only lead to unhappy owners and in turn, unhappy dogs. The last thing you'll want to do is re-home a dog, surrender them to a shelter, or much worse, put them to sleep, simply for exhibiting their breed's characteristic behaviors. It's always best to extensively research the breed you are considering, before purchasing or adopting a dog. This way, you'll be able to make the best, most informed decision possible. This is a very important decision so do not take it lightly.

Topic 2:
Choosing The Right Breeder

Once you have chosen the right breed of dog, the next step is to choose the right breeder. It is important to know that a good breeder will take the time to answer all of your questions, as well as ask you a list of their own. Ultimately it will be in your best interest to choose a breeder who interviews you as much as you interview them.

The following list of questions will help you in your search to find the right breeder:

Does the breeder breed for show, good temperament or both?

Is this breeder more concerned with breeding for good looks or for good temperament? Are they focused on breeding a dog that is more comfortable in the show ring than in a family environment?

It is important to realize that not all breeders who breed for show can guarantee that their dogs will make good family pets. Some show dogs are just that; "Show Dogs", not family dogs.

Be sure to know what it is that you are most concerned with, and be sure you ask the right questions in order to get the best dog for you and your family.

Does the breeder offer a "temperament guarantee"?

A breeder who breeds for good temperament should be willing to guarantee that their puppies will be happy, friendly and eager to investigate the world around them.

They should also be willing to guarantee that their puppies will not be overly fearful or show aggression towards humans in the form of growling, barking, lunging or biting.

You want to be sure that your breeder can guarantee the temperament of all their puppies. The best way to get this guarantee is in writing. If your breeder is unwilling to offer you this guarantee, you may want to find yourself another breeder.

How many litters does the breeder produce per year?

In order to avoid doing business with a breeder who is more concerned with quantity than quality, be sure to ask how many litters he or she has available for purchase on a yearly basis. If the breeder has one or more females that they breed, be sure to ask them how many litters each female produces per year. A female that churns out 3 or more litters per year may be stressed and could produce litters of unhealthy puppies.

Ultimately, **be sure that the mother of the puppy you will be taking home is a healthy female who is not being bred all year long.**

What kind of environment are the puppies being raised in?

Choose a breeder who raises his or her puppies inside of their home, and in a clean, safe environment. When a breeder raises his or her puppies inside of their home, the puppies are often exposed to the normal sights and sounds of home life. Having these opportunities will help prepare them for the transition into your home. A puppy that is raised in a structure separate from a home may not be given such exposure, and as a result may be easily frightened by anything and everything that is normal to home life.

Does the breeder safely expose the puppies to a crate, a car or the outside world?

The more of the outside world the puppy has been exposed to, the better. It will be much easier to housetrain a puppy if the breeder has trained them to be comfortable with being inside of a crate prior to going home with you. It will also be a lot easier for your car ride home and for future walks if the puppy has already had a pleasant introduction to cars and the outside world- and should therefore show little to no anxiety about being exposed to either.

Does the breeder provide a health record for each puppy?

The breeder should provide each new owner with a list of shots the puppy has already received as well as a list of those he or she will need in the near future.

This is important information that you will have to provide to your vet at your puppies' first wellness visit. Without it, your vet will have no history of your puppy's medical care.

What kind of health guarantee does the breeder offer?

A one-year health guarantee in writing is what you should ask for. A good breeder should be willing to offer this because he or she is confident in the good health of all their puppies. If your breeder is unwilling to offer you this guarantee, you may want to find yourself another breeder.

Does the breeder screen puppies for genetic diseases and guarantee that they will be free of genetic diseases that are common to their breed?

This is especially important when choosing a breed that is prone to joint, ligament, eye and/or respiratory problems.

You want to be sure that your breeder can guarantee the health of their puppies, and the best way to get this guarantee is in writing. Again, if your breeder is unwilling to offer you this guarantee, you may want to find yourself another breeder.

Will the breeder provide you with the names and numbers of people they have sold puppies to in the past year or two?

This is especially important because you will want to talk to several owners who have previously purchased a puppy from this breeder to find out if the breeder is in fact breeding healthy, happy puppies with good temperaments. These people are living with the dogs that this breeder has bred and they will be able to provide you with valuable unbiased information.

At what age does the breeder release a puppy to his or her new owner?

Eight to ten weeks is when most puppies are released to their new homes. Do not choose a breeder who releases their puppies under eight weeks of age. A puppy that is taken away from his or her mother before eight weeks of age may lose out on valuable lessons that he or she could have learned from their mother and littermates.

If you are unable to keep your puppy for one reason or another, will the breeder like "The First Right of Refusal"?

Always choose a breeder who will be willing to take back one of their own puppies should you need to re-home him or her at any time for any reason. Provided that the puppy has been properly cared for and has not been abused in any way, the breeder should always be willing to help by providing this type of assistance for the life of the dog.

Will the breeder be willing to provide you with advice and/or support after you have taken your puppy home?

A breeder can be a valuable asset to a new dog owner. After all, they are the ones who can give you the most information about your new puppy. Always look to choose a breeder who is willing to provide phone support and help guide you through the first few months of raising a puppy.

Finally, when making his very important decision, don't be lured by an elaborate website full of adorable pictures, or the pressure tactics of a pushy breeder. Choosing a breeder based on those factors may lead to disaster. Instead, choose a breeder based upon their answers to these questions. If a breeder seems annoyed that you are asking all the right questions, then hang up or walk away. A good breeder will always be happy to answer all of your questions, knowing that their puppy will be going to a responsible, well-informed owner who has done their homework.

Topic 3:
Acquiring Your Puppy

Another important decision is whether to choose a breeder you can drive to, or a breeder who will fly your puppy to you. Bear in mind that choosing a breeder you can drive to will afford you many wonderful opportunities. For instance, if you are able to visit the breeder, you should be able to see the environment in which the puppies are being raised. Are the surroundings clean and warm? Are the puppies being raised in a home and being exposed to all the normal things that he or she will be exposed to in your home, or are they being raised in an isolated area, separate from the breeder's home? Are the puppies being safely introduced to children, men and women? If a young puppy has been raised around men, women and children, they certainly should not be fearful of one or the other when it comes time to acclimate to you and/or your family.

If you are able to drive to the breeder, you should also be able to meet the puppies' parents. It's always best if you are able to meet both the mother and the father of the puppy when possible. Meeting both parents will give you a better idea of what kind of dog you will be getting, once your puppy matures into adulthood. For instance, if one of the parents is fearful or aggressive, there's a pretty good chance your puppy may show fearful or aggressive tendencies, if not immediately, then possibly later on, when they mature into adulthood. If Lori and Kurt had met Princess' parents, they would have discovered that her mother was a fearful poodle, while her father exhibited aggressive tendencies toward strangers. For Princess' breeder, looks were more important than temperament. Unfortunately, this is what attracted Lori to Princess' breeder in the first place. The minute she saw the gorgeous mother, the stoic father and their adorable puppies on the Breeder's website, she immediately called and reserved a puppy, without doing her research. Lori had no idea what questions to ask the breeder, to guarantee she was getting a good, healthy puppy and one who's temperament was well suited to both her and Kurt's lifestyle and expectations.

Choosing a breeder you can drive to will also afford you the luxury of visiting the litter and meeting the puppies first hand, to help you choose the puppy that is truly right for you. If the breeder has pre-selected a puppy for you, make sure that you have a few visits with that particular puppy, to be sure it's temperament is in fact a good fit for you and or your family. On the other hand, if you have the pick of the litter, just remember that the first puppy that comes bounding up to you may not be the best puppy for you. For instance, if you are looking for a laid back puppy, the first one that comes running up to you, may not be the one you want. In a litter of puppies, the first one that approaches you may be the alpha of the litter and this puppy will not likely be laid back. Often times, the alpha is used to going after what he or she wants and working hard until they get it. Because Lori and Kurt were unable to visit Princess' litter, they were unable to see that Princess was in fact the alpha dog, who persistently always got what she wanted. In her mind, everyone else's needs came second to hers. When choosing a puppy, always be sure to evaluate the temperaments of all the puppies in the litter. If you want a laid back dog, it may be wise to take a closer look at the puppy that is third, fourth or fifth to come up to greet you. Obviously, if the litter is smaller and you do not have many to choose from, just be aware that the first one to come barreling up to you, may be the alpha dog and that dog will come with their own unique set of personality traits.

In testing the temperament of a puppy, try using a simple key drop test. This is where you drop a set of keys near the puppy you are interested in and watch how he or she reacts. Ultimately, you want a puppy that may be startled at first, but then quickly goes right up to the keys to investigate. Be leery of the puppy that gets startled by the keys and then refuses to approach them to investigate. This puppy may jump back and bark at the keys, or simply hide behind you, acting fearful of these strange, noisy, foreign objects. You want a puppy that exhibits curiosity, as well as self-confidence. You don't want a puppy that is skittish and fearful. You may not even have to do the key drop test to see that a puppy seems overly shy. This puppy may be very hesitant to approach you and may even need to be carried to you by the breeder. Do not begin to think that this is cute. This shy puppy may grow up to be a skittish nightmare like Princess. Always be sure that the puppy you have chosen, or the puppy that has been chosen for you, willingly and easily walks up to you on their own four feet for a greeting. If the breeder chooses to show you only the puppy she has hand picked for you and not the other littermates or the puppy's mother, then be a bit cautious. Being able to see the entire litter and especially the mother, will give you a better overall opinion of the temperament of the litter. If all the other puppies are outgoing and friendly, that will be a good sign. On the other hand, if several of the puppies are shy, you should move forward with caution. Again, meeting the mother of the litter will be a good idea but may have to be done separate from the puppies, to avoid challenging her motherly, protective instincts.

If a breeder will not allow you the freedoms previously mentioned, then consider walking away. Not only should you be able to have a say in choosing the puppy that will be a part of your life for the next ten to fifteen years, but you should be given as much information about the puppy and his or her parents, in order to make the best, most educated decision possible.

If for some reason you have no choice but to choose a breeder who must fly your puppy to you, consider either paying extra to have the puppy flown in the coach section of the plane, or better yet, fly to the breeder and escort the dog back home with you. Flying to the breeder will allow you to make a first hand assessment of the breeder and his or her facility, before you fully commit to purchasing the puppy.

Topic 4:
10 Red-Flag Behaviors In Puppies

The following is a list of behaviors to be especially watchful of when bringing home a new puppy. Not only can these behaviors be extremely difficult to manage, but also they can be especially problematic when exhibited by a puppy under three months of age. Puppies this young should be silly, naïve, good-natured and interested in investigating the world around them. They shouldn't be anxiety ridden, overly fearful or aggressive.

Should you witness one or more of the following behaviors in your puppy, please seek the guidance of a professional dog trainer and or the assistance of your veterinarian.

Extreme Anxieties

These puppies may get startled easily, act overly cautious or exhibit avoidance behaviors around new people and things. A puppy with extreme anxieties may seem frightened by anything and everything around them.

Demonstrates Aggressive Tendencies

Aggression may take the form of growling, nipping, lunging or barking intensely at humans or other animals in the home. These puppies may also aggressively guard things like food, bones, toys or a particular human within the home.

Extremely Needy and Demanding Behaviors

Overly needy puppies may use excessive vocalizations to demand attention from their humans. These puppies are persistent in using *nuisance- behaviors* to get what they want. Owners of these puppies will find that, no matter how much they do for their puppy, it is not enough to make them happy or convince them to relax.

Inability To Be Left Alone

These puppies are unable to tolerate being left alone. When they are, in fact, forced to face this challenge, they may bark or whine uncontrollably; urinate or defecate due to heightened anxiety; self mutilate to displace stress; or even destroy household items like furniture, blinds, windowsills or door jams.

Not Crate Trained

A crate is a very important tool in the house training process; it is also an important tool in teaching a puppy frustration- tolerance. Being confined in a crate can be a very difficult thing for some puppies especially if they have never been exposed to one before being handed over to you. A puppy that is not comfortable with confinement will often exhibit excessive and overly dramatic vocalizations once placed inside a crate. This will often be difficult for most owners to work through and could result in a dog that is extremely difficult to housetrain and/or impossible to leave alone in a home.

Uses Crate As A Toilet

These puppies are often from pet stores or puppy mills and have no choice but to tolerate urine and feces in their living environment. They are usually raised in an area of confinement where they eliminate on wire flooring or on an absorbent material like pee pads or paper shavings. Essentially, these puppies are trained to poop and pee where they sleep. Eliminating in their crate makes perfect sense to them. The other downside to this type of behavior is that these puppies may then learn to consume their own feces and/or the feces of other dogs they are confined with. Regrettably, when a puppy develops a taste for poop, they may carry this addiction into adulthood, and this could lead to health issues in some dogs.

A crate is like a puppies' personal den. For a wild dog, a den is a place to sleep, hide and raise young. It is not a place to soil. Because a dog's natural instinct is to keep their den clean, a puppy should not want to soil in their crate. Unfortunately, a puppy that repeatedly eliminates in their crate will not only be very difficult to housetrain but the behavior may become difficult, if not impossible to break. A crate can be a valuable tool in the housetraining process because it should be the one place where your puppy is guaranteed to not poop or pee. Without this guarantee you can bet that the whole house will be fare game for your puppies' eliminations.

Excessively Urinates

Be aware that when a puppy repeatedly pees 4 or more times an hour. This may signal a possible urinary tract infection. If you suspect your puppy is suffering from a urinary tract infection, be sure to visit your veterinarian for an accurate diagnosis and early treatment.

Exhibits Lethargic Behavior

A puppy that is suffering from a health problem may not be interested in playing or eating. These puppies may even exhibit excessive vomiting and/or diarrhea. If your puppy demonstrates such behavior, immediately visit your veterinarian for an accurate diagnosis and treatment.

Non-Stop Scratching, Licking or Chewing on Self

This could be an indication that your puppy is suffering from an infestation of mites, mange or fleas. It could also be a signal that he or she may have a food- related allergy. It could also mean that your puppy is having an allergic reaction to something in its environment such as seasonal pollen, lawn pesticides, rug cleaner or the cleaning agent used to clean his or her crate and/or bedding.

Excessive Water Consumption

This behavior could be an indication of renal or liver problems.

Liver disease is one of the top five causes of death in dogs and the warning signs should be taken very seriously. Unfortunately for most dogs, the symptoms of liver and kidney problems often go unnoticed and undiagnosed until they reach a critical life-threatening stage.

If you are concerned about your puppy's water consumption, be sure to get him or her checked out by your veterinarian.

Topic 5:
Housetraining Your Puppy

Housetraining your puppy is an absolute must and the process should begin as soon as you take ownership of your new little bundle of joy. Before leaving a breeder's house or a shelter, be sure to give your puppy the opportunity to eliminate. This may be your puppy's first time in a car, so be aware that a full bladder and a stressful experience could cause your puppy to eliminate in your vehicle or in his or her crate. The next important step in the housetraining process is when you arrive home with your puppy. As soon as most owners get their puppy home, they immediately rush them inside to show them all the cute toys and treats they have waiting for them. Unfortunately, most anxious owners forget about their puppy's need to eliminate, especially after a stimulating car ride. By bringing them straight into the house, owners are basically telling their new puppy "Welcome to your new home! Feel free to pee or poop anywhere you'd like." Instead of heading straight into the house, you should leash your new puppy, unload them from your vehicle and escort them straight into the yard. Let their first pee and or poop be in your yard, not on your kitchen or living room floor. Do not head inside until they have eliminated in your yard. Once they have done their business, now you may bring them inside. Upon entering the house, do not simply unleash your puppy and allow him or her to go wandering unsupervised throughout the home. Instead, bring them right into the kitchen and let them investigate this room first. It will be a good idea to have this room gated off from the rest of the house. By doing this, you will be preventing your puppy from wandering, having unsupervised accidents and developing a preference for eliminating indoors. The best way to prevent this from happening will be to limit your puppy to a single room and in doing so, set them up for success. If you are welcoming an older dog into your home, it will be wise to follow these same steps. Bear in mind that just because an older dog is said to be housetrained, doesn't mean they are housetrained to the new environment they are entering into.

The next thing to do, once you bring your puppy inside, will be to set a timer. The amount of time you put on the timer, will depend on how old your puppy is. For instance, if you are bringing home an eight-week old puppy, it will be wise to set an egg timer or the timer on your microwave or phone for thirty-five minutes. When the timer goes off, take your puppy outside to go pee. Repeat this process over and over and over again throughout the day until it's time to go to bed. You will follow a timer method anytime you are awake and in the house and continue to use it for the next six months, or until your puppy is fully housetrained.

One exception to the rule is when your puppy decides to take a mid-day nap and is sleeping when the timer goes off. At this point, disregard the timer and simply wait until their nap is over. As soon as they wake, bring them outside as quickly as possible to eliminate. Whenever a puppy wakes up from a nap, be sure to get them right outside to go to the bathroom. Delaying their exit, while you run around the house looking for your shoes, hat or coat, may result in an accident. Instead, have everything you'll need to go outside, right by the door.

Another exception to the rule is when you leave the house to run errands. You will not have to observe the timer method anytime you are away from the home. Just be sure to let your puppy eliminate outside before leaving them alone in their crate. Also, try not to leave a new puppy in his or her crate for more than one or two hours at a time. If you are away for more than two hours, your new puppy may be forced to eliminate in his or her crate. If this happens, you may be starting a trend that could lead to your puppy using his or her crate as an out-house and this would not be good.

Another instance when you will not have to observe the timer method is at night, when you have gone to bed. The reason why you do not have to use the timer method while you are asleep is because when the house shuts down and everyone goes to bed, then the environment becomes less stimulating to your puppy and his or her bladder. On average, an eight-week-old puppy should be able to hold themselves for four to six hours at night without having to eliminate. The best way to assure that you get a decent night's sleep is to try and take your puppy out for his or her last outing as late in the evening as possible. The later you take them out, the less likely they will have to go to the bathroom in the middle of the night.

Fortunately, as the weeks progress, the duration of time between pee breaks, during the day and at night, will get longer and longer. If you started out setting your timer for thirty-five minutes when your puppy was eight weeks old, then simply add five or ten minutes extra with each passing week, to adjust for their growing bladder size and strength. For example, by the time your puppy is fourteen weeks old, you may be setting your timer for one hour and thirty minute intervals throughout the day and getting your puppy to sleep through the night because he or she no longer has to eliminate as frequently as they did when they were just eight weeks old.

When the timer goes off and you take your puppy outside, be sure to remember a few important rules. Once outside, do not stare directly at your puppy. You may steal a quick glance, but do not make direct eye contact. The reason for doing this is because you do not want to give your puppy unnecessary attention at this time. You want your puppy to find that you are offering them nothing but a short phrase, like "Do your business," and nothing else. If we give them excessive eye contact, we may distract them from the task at hand. They may forget all about peeing and think they are outside to play with you. Another reason to refrain from making direct eye contact with your puppy, when you are trying to get them to eliminate outside, is to give them privacy. Puppies and dogs in general, like to have a bit of privacy while they do their business. Think about the puppy that sneaks off into another room in the house to eliminate. They sneak off, so they can have a private moment. If you give your puppy a bit of privacy while outside, they may pee or poop quicker, because they feel more comfortable. Another aid you may want to use in the house training process is a twenty-foot cotton training lead (not a retractable leash). For some puppies, avoiding eye contact is not enough.

They want more privacy. They prefer to have a bit of distance between you and them in order for them to feel comfortable about eliminating. Once your puppy finds a spot to go and begins the act, do not say a word. You do not want to interrupt them while they are eliminating. Instead, simply look away, say nothing and get a treat ready. Once they are done, then it's time to celebrate. Tell them how amazing they are with excessive verbal praise and deliver them a small food reward on the spot. Make them feel as if they just did something truly amazing. Give them a reason to repeat this behavior outside, over and over and over again. Always be sure to give your dog a food reward as close to the act as possible, so they know what they are being rewarded for. If you wait until you get inside to give your puppy a food reward, then he or she will think you are rewarding them simply for coming inside, not for eliminating indoors. Once inside, feel free to give your puppy supervised playtime in a gated area like the kitchen until the timer goes off for the next outing. Please note that if you are welcoming an older dog into your home, be sure to follow the above suggestions, to ensure a successful housetraining experience, as they transition to their new life in your home.

When it's time to come back inside with your puppy, don't forget to reset your timer. If you are able to get into the habit of resetting your timer throughout the day, you are setting your puppy up for success. By getting them outside to pee on a consistent basis you will limit the number of mistakes they have inside your home. The goal is to get them outside before their bladder gets so full, that they lose control and have an accident. It also may be a good idea for you to keep a poop log. A poop log will allow you and anyone else in your household, to better gauge when your puppy may need to go poop throughout the day. Instead of it being a guessing game, you can use a log to chart their poop cycle, reduce accidents and increase chances for success.

Now, if for some reason, you take your puppy outside to eliminate and they do not go, simply take your puppy back inside and put them right into their crate. You do not want to allow a puppy with a full bladder to wander around inside your home. Instead, escort or carry them inside and put them right into their crate for twenty minutes. At the end of the twenty minutes, take your puppy right outside to try again. Refrain from eye contact, give them their bathroom prompt ("Do your business"), and get ready to reward them if and when they go. If they still won't go, then simply take them back inside and put them into their crate for yet another twenty minutes. You may find that outdoor conditions like rain, snow or cold weather, challenge your housetraining program. If these conditions make it difficult for your puppy to eliminate outside, do not fold and give them the option to go inside. Instead, use the crate and the twenty-minute rule to prevent your puppy from eliminating indoors. If we limit a puppy's options, we limit their ability to fail.

If at any time your puppy has a mistake inside your home, be sure to clean it up with an enzyme-neutralizing product. Do not use any product containing bleach or ammonia. These two ingredients will only aggravate the enzyme left behind in your puppy's pee or poop. If this enzyme is aggravated, it will make the spot smell even stronger to your puppy's nose. It will be like creating a bull's eye for your puppy's nose. It may smell clean to your nose, but to your puppy's nose, it says, "Go here, this is where you went before." If your puppy has a mistake on your hardwood floor, a solution of fifty percent water and fifty percent white vinegar will work great to not only clean your floor, but neutralize the odor to your puppy's nose.

Until your puppy is fully housetrained, do not allow them to roam unsupervised in your home. A puppy that is allowed to remain in a room unsupervised may take advantage of the privacy and eliminate in that room. Anytime a puppy cannot be given full supervision, they should be put into their crate. For instance, if you need to go downstairs to do laundry, go outside to get the mail or jump into the shower, you should put your puppy in his or her crate until you can return and provide full supervision of their activities. Do not look at the crate as a cruel place to put your puppy. It is a valuable tool in the housetraining process. It should be used to set your dog up for success. What is cruel is to not use a crate and to allow your puppy to roam throughout the home and eliminate wherever they choose. By doing this, you are training your puppy to eliminate indoors, and eventually they will receive punishment for a behavior you have trained them to do.

Housetraining is an ongoing process that usually continues until a dog is anywhere from six to twelve months old. The more diligent and consistent you are with sticking to a successful routine, the quicker your puppy will become housetrained. The more mistakes you make in the process, the more mistakes your puppy will make and the longer it will take to housetrain them. Be sure that everyone in your household gets involved with housetraining and above all, set your puppy up for success by remaining consistent in your housetraining program.

Topic 6:
Dos & Don'ts

Once a dog has been placed in your care, it is now your responsibility to help guide them through your world. The following is a list of suggestions that may help you in fulfilling your duty as teacher and translator:

Do teach your dog that human skin is fragile. Dogs should never be allowed to chew or teeth on human skin. If dogs are allowed to believe that human skin is tough, then what will stop them from using your fingers or hands as chew toys? Dogs should be provided with plenty of legal chew options of varying sizes, textures and materials. Providing your dog with plenty of things to chew, will help to discourage destructive chewing around your home, as well as give them an outlet for teething or bottled up energy.

Do teach your dog to be comfortable with riding in a car. Often times, dogs make negative associations with cars because of what they represent. A car can take them away from their mother and littermates and the only world they have known. Cars can also take them to the vet's office, where they get shots and experience stress. Don't just teach your dog that cars are bad. Teach them that cars can transport them to great fun. Let the number of car rides to the park to play, or to the beach to run in the surf, far outweigh the number of car rides to the vet's office. Unfortunately, the older the dog, the more difficult it may be to change their opinion of a car ride. Patiently try to work your dog through any phobia they may have in relation to cars, by replacing their negative memories with lots and lots of positive ones.

Do teach your dog to tolerate being groomed. The key to getting your dog to tolerate being groomed is to make it a good experience. Try providing your dog with a distraction like a treat dispensing toy stuffed with peanut butter or cheese. Let your dog lick at the peanut butter or cheese, while you slowly and gently groom them. If they have something delicious to focus their attention on, then they may sit fairly still and tolerate being groomed more easily.

Do teach your dog to be comfortable with walking on leash. Get your dog comfortable with a leash by attaching it to their collar or harness and then toss treats in front of them. Let them drag the leash behind them while in a gated area like the kitchen or living room. By focusing their attention on finding and eating the delicious treats, they will be less likely to think about and/or be bothered by the leash they are dragging behind them. There is no need to hold the leash, just let it drag behind them, while they chase after the treats. Once they feel completely comfortable with dragging a leash around, try picking up the leash and walking your dog around the house and then around the yard. Be sure to progress slowly with this task. Do not rush your dog and above all, do not make the mistake of carrying your dog, because getting them to walk on leash seems too difficult. You are doing your dog no good by carrying them around. If anything, you are doing them a disservice, by not teaching them a basic fundamental skill. Make this lesson a priority, not just for your dog's benefit, but for yours as well. After all, that ten- pound puppy may become a hundred pound dog and at that weight, a leash will become a must.

Do know how to pet your dog correctly. This may sound funny, but all too many people have no idea that dogs do not like being petted on the crown of their head. Dogs are body language communicators who try to communicate this dislike to us by flinching, squinting or ducking their head. I often ask people if they have ever encountered a dog, who upon greeting them, proceeds to shove his or her head between their legs. I then explain that a dog does this, because if you do not have access to their head, then you can't pet them somewhere they do not want to be petted. Dogs try to tell us so much with body language, but unfortunately, most of us just don't get it. Head petting is not only annoying to most dogs, but it is offensive to others as well. For instance, a dog that has a tendency to be aggressive or overly dominant, may interpret your hand going over his or her head, as a challenge. For these dogs, such an act is not acceptable and may result in them lunging backwards to bark at you, or worst-case scenario, result in them trying to bite you. I will often try to warn adults and especially children, of the potential hazards of patting a dog on the crown of their head, because petting the wrong dog incorrectly could have serious consequences. Another down side of petting a dog on the top of their head, can be seen in the come recall. If you call your dog to come to you and all they get as a reward for doing so, is a big hard pet on the crown of their head, then what will be their motivation to keep coming to you when called? When people say, "My dog just won't come when called," I always ask them how they reward their dog for their obedience. If they tell me they give them a loving head pet, I explain that this may be part of the problem. There obviously will be some dogs who just love to be petted on the crown of their head, but the point in mentioning this in the dos and don'ts section, is to speak up for those dogs who dislike it and point out how petting some dogs this way, may result in negative consequences.

Do reward all appropriate behavior. Give your dog a reason to repeat an action that you approve of. Why else would a dog choose to sit quietly at your feet for attention, when they could jump up on you to get what they want? Why would a dog choose to walk nicely on leash, when they could pull to get where they want to go faster? Why would a dog lay down in the back seat of a running car, when they could jump in the front seat and ride in your lap? Why, because they have been taught that sitting quietly for attention, walking nicely on leash or riding in the back seat of a moving vehicle, not only makes you feel good, but makes them feel good as well. Always reward a behavior that you approve of by using either food treats, verbal praise or both. Make them feel good about doing something you like. Common sense says that if a dog truly enjoys doing something because it has good benefits, then they're going to be more willing to do it over and over again without hesitation. If your dog makes good decisions, be sure to reward them for their good behavior.

Do be sure to teach your dog basic commands. Teaching your dog basic commands such as sit, down, stay, come, leave it and drop it are essential in order to communicate your house rules. A dog should know that boundaries and limitations not only exist but also are enforced in their environment. In order for a dog to see you as a leader and someone worth listening to, you must have house rules established and they must understand and respect them. *It's not mean to enforce house rules. What is mean is to expect them to follow the house rules when they don't even know what the house rules are.* The irony is that the owners, who are unwilling to take the time to train their dogs, are often the ones doing the most complaining about their dog's bad behaviors. Why would a dog respect or even listen to you, if you've made it clear that you have no house rules for them to obey? With no house rules you have no authority and should not expect your dog to listen to you or obey your requests.

Do teach your dog to feel comfortable and tolerate being in his or her crate. This is especially important for a dog that has never been introduced to a crate before. Once it's time to introduce your dog to their crate, put the crate on the floor, open its door and try hiding some treats inside the rear of the crate. This will encourage him or her to go completely inside and investigate the crate. Do not introduce your dog to a crate by just shoving him or her inside and shutting the door. Let him or her go in and out freely for several hours, before shutting the door for the first time. Do not simply wait to put your dog in his or her crate for the first time at bedtime. If you do this, you are asking for trouble and a sleepless night. Instead, give him or her a chance to get used to the crate for several hours throughout the day. Also, be sure not to acknowledge barking or whining while they are in the crate. Unless the vocalization is an indication that they needing to eliminate, it must be ignored. Try putting a blanket over three sides of a crate to reduce your ability to sneak a peak at them when they are whimpering, whining or barking. Be aware that a dog may be using vocalizations as a simple plea for your help. If they make their request sound urgent enough, maybe you will come to their rescue and remove them from their crate. Again, provided their vocalizations are not an indication of needing to eliminate, then the noise must be completely ignored. You must not look at them, talk to them or touch them while they are vocalizing in their crate. You must let your dog cry themselves to sleep without your intervention.

Eventually, your dog will learn that vocalizing will not make the crate door open and the duration of the noise will decrease to the point of elimination.

Don't teach your dog that vocalizations will make good things happen. Don't let your dog think that a whimper a whine or a bark will get them your attention. If your dog thinks that whining works to get you to look at them, then what's to say they won't escalate the demand to a bark, to make their request for attention even louder and more urgent. Remember that when a dog whines or barks for attention, they are hoping to get you to make eye contact with them. If they see that you are interested in what they have to say, then most likely they will continue with their vocalizations and continue using noise to get attention, in hopes of getting their demands met. Unfortunately, most owners unknowingly turn their dogs into endurance barkers, when they try ignoring the whimpering and/or barking for a few minutes but then give in to the noise when they decide they just can't take it anymore. Giving in will only teach them to bark louder and longer, knowing that eventually they will wear you down and get what they want.

Do teach your dog to tolerate frustrating situations. Frustration tolerance is often a very difficult lesson for most owners because it requires them to develop a tough shell. Most dogs will attempt to whine, howl or bark until they get what they want. Often times, this may go on for hours and for most owners, the urge to give them what they want, just to get them to quiet down, is overwhelming. Unfortunately, this approach will only lead to a dog that has not been taught to self-sooth without human intervention. Owners who do not teach their dog frustration tolerance, for one reason or another, will often have a dog who will not tolerate being in a crate, being alone and/ or not getting their way. Teaching a dog to tolerate frustrating situations is a life skill. It's something that will help them to cope and ultimately to settle themselves down and relax. It's sad to think of a dog whining all night and working themselves into a drooling mess because they have been taught that if they vocalize long enough, their demands will eventually be met by the owner, who will fold and give them what they want. Unfortunately, these are the same dogs who will eventually get yelled at or physically punished for a behavior they have been trained to do and that is to rely on vocalizations to get their needs met.

Do provide your dog with plenty of exercise. Lack of exercise can lead to a number of behavioral problems like hyperactivity, destructive chewing, digging or even excessive barking. Having pent up energy can frustrate a dog, especially if they are a breed that demands a lot of exercise. Letting your dog out into your backyard while you are inside, is not exercising your dog. A dog must be given the chance to walk or run several times a day, in order to fulfill their exercise needs. It is essential to provide for your dog's basic needs and exercise is certainly one of those basic, but very important needs. If you find it difficult to give your dog adequate exercise each day, consider hiring a dog walker or enroll in a doggie daycare. Remember, a tired dog is often a very well behaved dog, but an under exercised, frustrated dog, can turn your home upside down.

Don't teach your dog that demanding behaviors will make good things happen. Do not teach your dog that demanding behaviors such as staring, pawing, whining or barking at you, will get them your attention. It's very rude behavior in the dog world for a lower ranking pack member to make demands of a higher-ranking member. However if you allow your dog to think that they are in charge, then they will certainly feel free to boss you around with even seemingly minor demands. Even if you think the whining or whimpering or barking is cute at first, believe me it will not be very cute when the vocalizations get louder, longer and more frequent.

Don't teach your dog that fearful behavior will get them attention. THIS IS A BIG NO NO!!!! Giving your dog attention by either looking at them, talking to them or touching them when they are exhibiting fearful behavior, is like rewarding them for being afraid. For instance, dogs who learn that shaking will get their owners to look at them, talk to them and/or pick them up to coddle them, will use this tact more and more because it works. These dogs are constantly trying to figure out what works and what doesn't work to get them more and more attention and more and more control over their environment. Unfortunately, once they find something that works, they'll stick to it. Princess the Cockapoo was a prime example of how rewarding fearful behavior, can result in a nightmare of a dog. Not only is rewarding fearful behavior a bad idea, but it will impair your dog's ability to socialize as well. If you never force your dog to stand on their own four feet and tolerate new people, places and things, then they will never learn to socialize and enjoy themselves. Often times, these dogs are unable to cope with being away from their owners and may even develop separation anxiety. They will usually exhibit so much anxiety, that their owners feel guilty to even leave them alone in the house. As a result, the dog never has to tolerate being alone and/or away from their owner. The owners of these dogs have trained them to be this way and will forever be prisoners in their dog's anxiety ridden world.

As important as it is to ignore your dog when they exhibit fearful behavior, it is also equally important to recognize and reward bravery and non-anxiety based behaviors. For instance, it's much better to reward your dog for patiently sitting by your side waiting for attention, than to give attention to a dog that jumps on you anxiously demanding your immediate attention and affection. The best way to get your dog to abandon their anxieties is to stop fueling them. Stop rewarding them for acting fearful. Stop thinking that your attention will make these behaviors go away. In order to get your dog to change their behavior, you must change how you react to their actions. After all, they wouldn't be doing what they were doing, unless you were somehow encouraging and/or supporting their behaviors.

Don't ask your dog to do things. One of the biggest, most common mistakes is when owners ask their dog to do something. Instead of asking, owners should be telling their dog what to do. By telling them, the command takes on authority. By asking them, an owner is giving the dog a choice. They haven't been commanded to do something, they have been asked and therefore, they have the option to ignore your request. The problem arises when your dog's safety is in jeopardy. If a dog is accustomed to being asked to do something and therefore accustomed to choosing between listening and not listening, then what happens when a dog escapes from his or her owner and runs toward a busy street. If the dog is used to ignoring commands, then that dog will most likely get hit by a car and possibly be killed. It's always best to set a dog up for success. A dog that is used to listening and obeying their owner will most likely have a far higher survival rate than a dog that continually chooses to ignore his or her owner's commands. Plain and simple, if you take the time to train your dog to listen and obey your commands, then you could very well be saving their life.

Do be careful at dog parks. Dog parks are not always full of happy, friendly dogs looking to have a good time. Instead, they can be a place where under socialized or aggressive dogs are allowed to wander off leash. Often times, these dogs will be looking to start trouble. These dogs use dog parks and dog gathering areas to hone their skills as bullies. Granted these dogs may be few and far between, but they are out there and owners should be aware that they could pose a threat to their dog. When at all possible, it is best to socialize with familiar dogs. Don't be so worried if the dogs are of different sizes and ages. What's most important is that they are friendly and have reliably good temperaments.

Do choose the right trainer to train both you and your dog. The trainer you choose should not only train your dog, but they should train you as well. He or she should also make dog training and dog ownership a fun and positive experience. Like everything else in life, you get what you pay for. Choosing the cheapest trainer or the trainer with the least amount of expe-rience may not be the best decision. You want a trainer who has a great deal of experience under his or her belt. You want a trainer who has seen it all and who's experience will allow them to problem solve through just about any challenge you throw their way. Also, be aware of the option to train your dog in a class environment or within the comfort of your own home. While some owners may prefer the socialization opportunities of a six to eight week group class, other dog owners may choose or need the personalized attention that an in-home private training session provides. Either way, by choosing to get your dog involved with a training program, you will be doing your dog a wonderful service and ultimately setting them up for a lifetime of success.

Topic 7:
Body Language In Dogs

Dogs are primarily ***body- language communicators***. They communicate what is on their mind through bodily displays. Dogs can easily tell what another dog is thinking because they "speak" the same language.

Just as important as it is for one dog to understand what another dog is trying to tell them, it is equally as important for a dog owner to understand this language as well.

The following is a helpful list of physical displays that all dog owners should understand and be on the lookout for in order to keep their own dog safe while out on a walk or at a dog park:

A relaxed and happy dog will make the following displays:

The dog's **body** will be relaxed, loose and wiggly
The dog's **tail** and rear end will wag from side to side
The dog's **mouth** will be open in what almost looks like a smile
The dog's **eyes** will look normal in size
The dog's **ears** will be held in their natural position
The dog's **hair** will lie flat against his or her body

A tense and unhappy dog will make the following displays:

The dog's **body** will be stiff
The dog's **tail** will be held high and may be wagging
The dog's **mouth** will be closed
The dog's **eyes** will show their whites
The dog's **head** will be held high and very still
The dog's **ears** will be raised up and slightly forward or slightly pulled back
The dog's **hair** may be raised over their shoulders or along their spine

A dog that is making a direct threat of aggression will make the following displays:

The dog's **body and tail** will be stiff
The dog's **head** will be held low
The dog's **ears** will be pinned back and flat against his or her head
The dog's **lip** will be raised to show teeth accompanied by growling
The dog's **eyes** will appear big and bugged out in a hard stare

Topic 8:
The Good, The Bad & The Ugly of Dog Parks

While a dog park can be a great place to socialize and exercise your dog, it may also be a place where dogs are bullied, abused and possibly attacked.

The following are some important behaviors for you to be aware of in order to keep your dog safe the next time you visit a dog park:

Good Play Behaviors At Dog Parks

One dog play-bowing to another
One dog pawing the air in front of another dog
One dog giving a whole body wiggle to another dog
One dog turning and pushing their butt into the face or side of another dog
Play wrestling where dogs take turns being on top
Play chasing where dogs take turns as the chaser, and then they become the chased
Playing fetch where dogs happily take turns retrieving a ball

Bad Play Behaviors At Dog Parks

A dog repeatedly tries to put their head, mouth or paw on the back of another dog's neck to show dominance

One dog snaps, snarls or shows their teeth repeatedly to other dogs

One dog runs around with the hair raised on the back of their neck

One dog barks non-stop at the other dogs

One dog obsessively and aggressively herds the other dogs

One dog aggressively and continuously mounts other dogs

Topic 9:
Owners Who Will Not Lead

With dog ownership comes a great responsibility. The responsibility of teaching your dog to find joy living in your world, with you as the leader. Unfortunately many dog owners make the mistake of living in a world where their dog is the one calling all the shots. Owners who live like this are often slaves to their dog's never-ending demands. Although some owners may be happy living like this, the dogs themselves, are usually anything but happy. Dogs who live without leaders are usually dogs that exhibit some of the most problematic behavioral issues. These dogs usually have no real ability to tolerate frustrating situations. They live without boundaries or limitations in their environment and they usually get everything they want, when they want. These are the dogs that unfortunately have no clear leader to guide them through life. The sad thing about a dog living in a world without a leader, is that the dog will usually be forced to assume the leadership role and in doing so, take on a job they are completely unfit for.

Dogs without leaders will often be more reactive to their environment through vocalizations and have difficulty coping with strangers in or around their home. These dogs may also over-react to being left alone by barking, soiling or destructively chewing as a way to vent their frustrations. A dog that is in the leadership position in the household, will not only have little to no respect for their owners, but for the owner's possessions as well. After all, if they are the leader of their environment, then anything and everything in that environment is theirs.

Not all dogs with owners who do not lead, will respond in this way, but often times a great deal of them will, out of sheer frustration. Like Princess, dogs that are in charge of their environment will often be extremely demanding of their owner(s) in order to get anything and everything they want. Unfortunately, what they want isn't always what they truly need.

Owners who choose to let their dogs be head of household, may think that they are giving them a wonderful gift, but truth be known, it is actually a punishment. Whether it's a dog from a breeder or a dog from a shelter, dogs don't come into a human environment wanting to lead. They may come into a human environment wanting to have their needs met, but that doesn't mean they want the added burden of leadership. Unfortunately, when dogs are given too much of a good thing, it can often spell trouble, not just for them, but for those living around them as well. Owners caught in this predicament, will often make excuses for their dog's unruly behaviors, never really coming out and admitting that they see the behaviors as problematic. The problem is that by allowing the dog to exist without rules and boundaries, not only will the dog be problematic to his or her owners, but a potential hazard to outsiders as well.

Not all dogs will respond to a lack of leadership in the ways just discussed. Some dogs can be given the sun, the moon and the stars and not turn into a nightmare. These dogs are different from the ones who are given an inch and want a mile. These dogs can handle excess without a problem, even when their owners have abandoned their responsibility of providing leadership.

When you assume the responsibility of dog ownership, you owe it to your dog to provide them with the tools to succeed in life. You owe it to them to be their teacher and their leader. You should strive to be an owner who sets their dog up for success, not failure. You should want your dog to live a happy and healthy life and you should make every effort to prepare them for the world around them, through a commitment to training.

Topic 10:
Don't Make Your Dog's Problematic Behavior Someone Else's Burden

What many people don't realize, is that the decisions they make as dog owners, can greatly affect the lives and well being of so many. Case in point let me tell you about an experience I had not too long ago. While walking my dog Meagan, with my husband and daughters, we came across a dog that was out for more than just a leisurely stroll with his owners. This dog was a feisty little Jack Russell, who just about dragged the six-year-old boy who was attempting to walk him, up the sidewalk to greet us. The speed, at which this dog approached Meagan, indicated that he meant business. I wasn't overly concerned with the greeting, until the little boy's mother nervously said to the dog "Now Nicky be nice. Nicky be nice." Unfortunately for Meagan, these words fell upon his deaf ears and within only five seconds of greeting her, this little Jack Russell proceeded to launch himself at her neck. I quickly pulled Meagan backwards into the street, to avoid this little devil and to save Meagan from a visit to the vet's. Luckily for both of us, there were no cars coming when we darted out into the street, otherwise the situation could have become even more problematic for both of us. What was truly amazing was that even after her dog had obviously tried to attack Meagan, the owner had no idea what had just happened. It was as if she had closed her eyes during the altercation. Not only was she giggling, but so was her son. I couldn't believe she thought what had just happened was funny. Had she not realized that her dog had tried to attack my dog and could have killed us both, if a car had been coming down the street that we darted out onto? Was she that heartless or was she was just in denial? She saw Nicky as a sweet little dog that just wanted to give Meagan a kiss. She had no idea that her dog was a threat to other dogs. Quickly assuming that this woman was an inexperienced dog owner of an obviously problematic dog, I took a deep breath and asked her "Does your dog normally do this?" Giggling, she said, "Oh Nicky was just excited, she loves to play with other dogs." Clearly she was misinterpreting her dog's aggression as a rambunctious desire to be friendly. This was not the case however. When I tried to explain to her that her dog's behavior was not about being friendly, she laughed it off saying "Oh dogs will be dogs," and walked away.

Unfortunately, dog-on-dog aggression isn't the only problematic issue that needs addressing. Dog-on-human aggression is even more serious, but just as easily ignored by many dog owners.

One example that comes to mind, involved a Bichon Frise that I encountered at a local pet store, several years ago. While kneeling down to choose a toy for my dog, I was quickly approached by Missy and her owner. At first, I was so focused on the toys, that I didn't even see the little dog come racing up to me. Missy had caught me in a squatted position, so I was a bit vulnerable, being down on her level. My immediate reaction was to look at Missy's owner and ask her if the dog, which was now by my side, was friendly. She quickly assured me that she was very friendly and loved meeting new people. With that having been said, I reached out to let Missy smell my hand and rather than smell it, she opted to bite it. This little dog, whose owner had claimed she was so friendly, had just given me three small puncture wounds on my right hand. After jumping to my feet and shaking off the pain, all I could do was watch in disbelief, as Missy's owner proceeded to reprimand her dog by scooping her up to hug her and ask her why should would have done such a thing. Missy's owner was actually hugging her, acting as if Missy had been the victim of a dog attack. What was so shocking to me was not only had this woman allowed her dog to stalk me and then attack me, but that she lied about her dog being friendly. Missy's owner couldn't apologize enough, but unfortunately, the damage had already been done. With tears in her eyes, she explained that this had not been the first time that Missy had acted aggressively toward a stranger. She had actually done this nearly a dozen times, but had never broken skin on someone. Like so many other dog owners, Missy's owner had just hoped that the behavior would improve with time and with meeting more and more people. Unfortunately, this was not the way to handle a dog with aggressive tendencies. Missy's owner should have had a better handle on her dog's aggressive behavior and should not have been allowing her to victimize the general public. Missy's owner should have sought professional help, so as not to allow her dog's problematic behavior to become my problem.

What is often very frustrating, is not that a dog is aggressive, dominant or unskilled at socializing with other people or dogs, but that the dog's owner either doesn't see it as a problem, or just hopes that it will go away with time. Unfortunately, the more dogs or people these types of dogs meet, the more chances they will have to hone their bullying skills and ultimately, the more dogs and/or people they can possibly injure. This is no different than the dog owner who goes to the dog park, knowing that their dog is aggressive and by releasing the dog to run loose, the owner is actually allowing their dog to go on a hunt. Unfortunately, the hunt will involve finding another dog or human at the dog park to attack. *Shame on those owners who allow their dogs to threaten the safety and well being of other innocent dogs and/or humans.* Owners of these aggressive and problematic dogs should either seek professional assistance, to get a handle on their dog's aggressive tendencies, or just prohibit their dogs from interacting with other dogs and/or humans. Would you let your child run around in public with a concealed weapon to use at their leisure? Most likely not, so why would you let your dog use his or her aggressive behavior as their own secret weapon? As a dog owner, it is your responsibility to provide your dog with proper training, to not only set them up for success in your home, but out in public as well. Once again, if you do not have the time, resources, or know how to fix your dog's problematic behavior, either seek professional help from a trainer or re-think your decision to be a dog owner. Either way, don't be selfish and ignore the problem, only to make it someone else's burden.

Topic 11:
Top 10 Commandments

Socialize, Socialize, Socialize

Socialization allows your puppy to develop their interactive skills with other dogs as well as build their tolerance to new situations and environments. When socializing your puppy, choose activities that can be controlled in order to make the experience both fun and beneficial to your puppy. Without safe and extensive exposure to the world around them, your puppy could grow up to be a fearful, skittish, neurotic adult dog who would prefer to stay at home and hide rather than venture out into the real world to enjoy life with his or her family.

Socialization is an ongoing process that should continue right up to your puppies' first birthday. Just remember: the more people, places, things and dogs your puppy encounters, the more prepared they will be to navigate through this big, wide world.

Teach Your Dog The "House Rules"

The best time to teach your dog the "House Rules" is the day you bring them home. Be sure everyone in the house is in agreement on what rules to establish so as to avoid confusion for everyone-including the dog. The last thing you want is to have one house member teaching the dog that the couch is off limits, while another is inviting them up for a cuddle. This type of behavior will only confuse your dog and make the "House Rules" difficult to teach and enforce.

Teach Your Dog Basic Commands

All dogs should be taught the following basic commands:

"Sit; Stay; Lie Down; Come; Drop it; Leave it; Wait; and Quiet.

Not only will these commands allow you to better communicate your "House Rules," but they they will also help to protect your dog from danger. For instance, teaching your dog to "come" when called could prevent them from being hit by a car or sprayed by a skunk, or better yet- their obedience could enable them to enjoy off-leash privileges in the yard, at the beach or at the local park.

Crate Train Your Dog

As I mentioned earlier, introducing your dog to a crate is not just a good idea, it should be one of the first things you do as a new dog owner.

When your dog is properly crate trained, they will see their crate as a den and a place to retire to when they are exhausted or just want to be alone. It becomes a place where they can relax. Without a comfortable "den", your dog may not be able to settle down; they may wander throughout the home, restless and full of anxiety.

A crate is also a must when it comes to housetraining. Without a place of confinement, you will be setting your dog up for failure. If your new dog is allowed to wander, then they will most likely eliminate throughout the home. Instead, train your dog to feel comfortable with their crate and set them up for success.

Crate training your dog will also allow you to leave your home knowing that your dog is safe. A new dog or puppy that is not housetrained should never be allowed to have free run of your home. There are just too many things they could get into, too many things that could injure them and too many places they could go poop or pee.

Freedom should be an earned privilege that is granted as a reward for good behavior and one of the best ways to train your dog to achieve this success is through the use of a crate.

Not only can a crate be a beneficial tool in housetraining your puppy, it can also be essential when dealing with a dog that suffers from separation anxiety. For those dogs, confinement can be comforting and help to reduce stress by reducing their ability to roam and potentially damage the home and/or injure themselves. When dogs with separation anxiety are allowed to roam, they become more and more stimulated, more and more stressed and more and more agitated. By utilizing a crate, you increase the likely hood that a dog with separation anxiety will settle down and relax while you are away.

Teach Your Dog Frustration Tolerance

Teaching your dog to develop patience is a must. There will be countless situations when your dog will want to get their way immediately. If he or she has not been trained to deal with frustration, then we cannot expect them to handle it well. For instance, how can we expect to crate train a dog if we open the door and let them out each and every time they bark or scratch at the crate door? The dog inside the crate must learn to be patient. He or she needs to learn that all the barking, whining and scratching in the world will not make the door open. Instead, they will need to tolerate this frustrating situation and wait until you decide to open the door and let them out.

Dogs that have no patience may increase their level of demands until they get what they want. Sometimes the intensity of demands can go from frustration to rage and end with aggression. These dogs may get to the point where they may threaten to bite if they are unable to get what they want - when they want it. These dogs can be loud and obnoxious with their non-stop vocalizations; they can be over demanding, persistent and simply a nightmare to be around.

Teaching your dog to develop coping skills will help improve their ability to deal with frustration and frustrating situations. Although it may not be easy to deny a dog what they want when they want it, just know that by teaching them frustration tolerance, you are giving them one of the best gifts an owner can give their four legged friend.

Don't Teach Your Dog That Vocalizations Make Good Things Happen

Every dog owner should understand how important it is not to reward excessive vocalizations. When a young puppy whimpers and then gets rewarded by being looked at, picked up, kissed and/or hugged, he or she quickly learns that vocalizations make good things happen. The real problem arises when the whimper becomes a whine and then the whine becomes a bark and then the barking continues until the puppy gets everything he or she wants.

Ultimately, the best way to prevent your dog from becoming a nuisance barker is to not reward excessive and/or demanding vocalizations. Instead, reward your dog with verbal praise and/or treats when they choose to be quiet and calm. Do not reward the demanding behaviors, instead, reward the passive ones. Give your dog a reason not to yell and scream for your attention. Teach them that good things can come their way for acting calm, cool and collected.

Do Not Reward Your Dog For Anxiety Or Fearful Behaviors

Just as a dog can be inappropriately taught to use vocalizations to make good things happen, they can also learn to use fearful behaviors in the same manner. For instance, when a dog is startled by a loud noise he or she may exhibit a response that is based on surprise and/or fear. During this response, an owner should resist the temptation to respond to the dog's fear with sympathy: such as picking them up, or whispering soothing words to try and calm them. By doing this, you can bet the dog will register this response as a" feel good response" to his or her fearful behavior. In the dog's mind, a fearful display was addressed with love and attention, and this made them feel good. With this type of memory, why wouldn't a dog react with fear to make more good things come their way?

A dog may exhibit fear by tucking their tail between their legs, panting, shaking or nonstop barking in response to something they think they should be fearful of.

The real key to managing these fearful behaviors is by not supporting them with a sympathetic response. You must ignore these behaviors rather then give them positive attention. Instead of trying to comfort the dog, calmly leave the room, avoid eye contact, and/or place your dog in a safe environment like a crate until they calm down and abandon their anxiety. Once they do this you can approach them and give them as much love and attention as you want.

It will be essential that you exhibit restraint and above all, stay calm during this process. By not responding with anxiety or concern, it's like you're telling your dog "Hey I'm not reacting to that noise because I am not threatened or upset by it and neither should you be."

Supporting a dog's fearful displays with positive attention, will only increase the likelihood of them returning again and again and again. Instead, it is best to discourage fear and encourage bravery. Teach your dog that the way to get your attention is not by acting fearful but by acting calm, cool and collected.

Do Not Reward Your Dog For Physically Demanding Behaviors

When we teach a dog to rely on physical demands, then we are asking for trouble. Actions like: pawing at your arm or leg; nose nudging; nipping; or jumping to get attention are a few common physical demands that dogs exhibit. Giving positive attention to a dog's vocalizations or fearful behaviors is not smart, but giving positive attention to physical demands is dangerous. If you train your dog to physically touch you to get your attention, then innocent people may be in for a world of hurt. For instance, when the 100 pound Lab that has been rewarded for pawing at their owners for attention asks a 5-year-old child for attention by running their paw down the side of the child's face, then you know you made a big mistake in training your dog.

Dogs should never be rewarded for using physical demands, instead teach them once again that passive, calm behaviors are the key to making good things happen.

Always Provide Feedback For Your Dog's Behaviors

Owners need to understand that a dog needs to be given feedback for good and bad behavioral choices. It is just as important to reward a dog for lying quietly on his or her bed, as it is to teach them that jumping on guests is an inappropriate behavior. In order to get a dog to want to do something over and over again, you have to make it worth their while.

Owners must give their dog positive feedback, so the dog can feel about having done something. Give them reason to want to repeat a behavior. Ironically, most often, a dog will be given attention for a bad behavior and ignored for a good behavior. For example, a dog that is lying quietly on their bed waiting for the owner's attention will often be ignored, while a dog that jumps on his or her owner for attention will receive the owner's eye contact and most likely a verbal and physical response. If the passive behavior gets ignored and the physical, demanding behavior gets three forms of attention, what is the motivation to choose a passive behavior? There is none. This is how it becomes easy to train a dog to exhibit bad behaviors instead of good ones. Dogs who experience this type of feedback will often choose demanding behaviors that get lots of attention over passive behaviors that get ignored.

Some dogs will even tolerate extremely negative attention for exhibiting certain behaviors. These are usually dogs that only receive negative feedback. For them, negative attention is better than no attention at all.

The best way to prevent this from happening is to give dogs feedback for good as well as bad behaviors. Use verbal praise and food rewards to give them reason to repeat a behavior. Train them to know which behaviors they should give up on and which behavior they can feel good about repeating over and over again.

Provide For Your Dog's Exercise Needs

In order to make sure you are raising a happy and healthy dog, it is essential that you do your best to provide for the basic needs of your canine companion.

The first and most basic of those needs is exercise. For a puppy, the best forms of exercise are periods of play and short walks. The great thing about play is that when they get tired, they simply stop playing and take a break. Play allows puppies to exert themselves according to their own endurance level. When it comes to walks, remember to start off with short walks and slowly increase their duration and intensity over time. As a puppy gets older, he or she will not only develop the endurance to play longer, but also to walk further and enjoy more opportunities to exercise and socialize.

For adult dogs, exercise is an absolute must. While some breeds may have limitations on how much activity they can tolerate, most dogs will greatly benefit from a minimum of 30 minutes of aerobic activity per day. Taking your dog out for a quick walk around the block just isn't enough. Dogs need to run in order to truly burn off all the excess energy that gets built up from sitting around the house. Without adequate exercise, dogs can develop behavioral issues such as destructive chewing, barking, digging, inappropriate eliminations and hyperactivity. Be sure to take into consideration the exercise requirements of your breed of dog and do your best to meet those needs on a daily basis. Always remember that a tired dog is most often a happy, healthy and well-behaved dog.

Conclusion

Anyone can own a dog, but it takes a good owner, to own a good dog. It takes time, patience and a commitment to doing what's right. It's about being a good teacher, translator and guide. It's about learning, growing and showing your dog you love them by giving them the tools necessary to succeed in this world. It's about setting them up for success, by educating yourself, learning to recognize your dog's needs and fulfilling those needs to the best of your ability. It's not about turning a blind eye to a problem in hopes that it will go away. It's not about allowing a molehill to become a mountain. It's not about giving up and giving away. It's about taking on a job and taking that job seriously.

Dog ownership can be a wonderful experience, but at the same time, it can be a very challenging endeavor. Without the proper guidance, motivation and commitment, it can become a daunting task for some. Professional dog trainers serve a very important role and should be utilized. Don't be afraid to ask for help. Whether you enroll in a group training class, or choose to hire an in-home dog trainer, you are not just doing what's best for your dog, but you are doing what's best for you and/or your family. Whether you are a first time dog owner, or have had dogs your entire life, getting your dog involved in a training program is a must. Training allows you to bond, as well as open up lines of communication with your dog. Training will also allow you secure their safety and the safety of those he or she will come in contact with throughout their lifetime.

Ultimately, being a good dog owner is about leading as much as loving. It's about guiding your dog through this world in a way that allows them to feel safe and well cared for. Because knowing what to do can sometimes be half the battle of doing what's right, you can now move forward having learned what it takes to not just be a good owner but a great owner. As someone who has taken the time to read and absorb all that this book has to offer, you can now feel confident and well prepared to handle many of the challenges that dog ownership can offer. Now you have no excuses; you know what to do, so get out there and make the most of what you've learned and above all don't forget to HAVE FUN!

About The Author

Jill Keaton has been training dogs and their owners for the past thirteen years and is the owner of The Social Canine, a doggie daycare in Westford, MA.

As an in-home dog trainer, she has helped thousands of owners improve communication with their dogs and in turn, improve the quality of life they share together.

Jill currently lives in Littleton, MA, with her husband Jim, their two daughters and a twelve-year-old rescue dog, named Meagan.

CPSIA information can be obtained at www.ICGtesting.com
Printed in the USA
BVOW09s2119301214

381431BV00007B/76/P